CW01315577

BRUGES

COMPREHENSIVE TRAVEL GUIDE 2024

Explore History, Culture, Hidden Gems, Cuisine and Local Secrets in the Venice of the North – Packed with Detailed Maps & Travel Resources

BY

MICHAEL VIANNEY

Copyright © 2024 Michael Vianney. All rights reserved. The entirety of this material, encompassing text, visuals, and other multimedia elements, is the intellectual property of Michael Vianney and is safeguarded by copyright legislation and global agreements. No segment of this content may be replicated, shared, or transmitted in any form or via any medium without explicit written authorization from Michael Vianney. Unauthorized utilization, replication, or dispersal of this content may result in legal repercussions, encompassing civil and criminal penalties. For queries regarding permissions or additional information, kindly contact the author via the provided contact details in the publication or on the author's official page.

TABLE OF CONTENTS

MY EXPERIENCE IN BRUGES

As a seasoned traveler and avid explorer, I've roamed the globe in search of hidden gems and cultural treasures. Yet, amidst the countless destinations I've visited, there's one place that holds a special corner in my heart – the mesmerizing city of Bruges. Nestled in the heart of Belgium, this charming medieval town captivated my senses and left an indelible mark on my soul. My journey to Bruges was not merely a tourist expedition; it was a quest to uncover the essence of a city steeped in history and tradition. From the moment I set foot in its cobblestone streets, I was transported back in time to a bygone era of knights and merchants, where every corner revealed a story waiting to be told.

The first thing that struck me about Bruges was its unparalleled beauty. The city's well-preserved medieval architecture, adorned with intricate lace-like facades and towering spires, seemed straight out of a fairy tale. As I wandered through its labyrinthine alleys and picturesque squares, I couldn't help but marvel at the timeless elegance that permeated every corner. But Bruges is more than just a pretty face; it's a cultural powerhouse with a rich tapestry of art, music, and gastronomy. One of the highlights of my visit was exploring the city's world-class museums, which house masterpieces by renowned Flemish painters such as Jan van Eyck and Hans Memling. Each brushstroke seemed to whisper secrets of a bygone era, inviting me to delve deeper into the city's artistic heritage. Of course, no trip to Bruges would be complete without indulging in its culinary delights. From mouthwatering Belgian chocolates to crispy golden waffles, the city's gastronomic scene is a feast for the senses. I fondly remember savoring a warm bowl of moules-frites at a quaint bistro by the canal, the salty sea breeze mingling with the aroma of steaming broth – a culinary experience like no other.

But perhaps what struck me most about Bruges was its palpable sense of tranquility. Despite being a popular tourist destination, the city exudes a peaceful ambiance that is both soothing and rejuvenating. Whether I was strolling along the tranquil canals or basking in the sun-drenched courtyard of the Beguinage, I felt a profound sense of serenity wash over me, as if time itself had come to a standstill. Yet, amidst its serene beauty, Bruges pulsates with life and vitality. The city's vibrant cultural scene is a testament to its enduring spirit, with festivals, concerts, and events happening year-round. I was fortunate enough to witness the colorful spectacle of the Bruges Beer Festival, where locals and visitors alike came together to celebrate the rich brewing tradition that has been passed down through generations.

As I reluctantly bid farewell to Bruges, I couldn't help but reflect on the profound impact the city had on me. It was more than just a destination; it was a journey of self-discovery, a pilgrimage to the very heart of Europe's soul. In Bruges, I found not only beauty and history but also a sense of belonging – a feeling that I had stumbled upon a place where time stood still and dreams came to life. So, to all those who seek adventure and inspiration, I implore you – come and experience the magic of Bruges for yourself. Let its timeless charm and enchanting allure capture your heart and ignite your imagination. For in the cobblestone streets and gabled rooftops of this medieval marvel, you'll find not only a destination but a destiny waiting to be discovered.

WHY VISIT BRUGES?

Located in the heart of Belgium, Bruges beckons travelers with its timeless charm and enchanting allure. As a veteran explorer, I've had the privilege of wandering through its cobblestone streets and gazing upon its medieval marvels, and I can attest that Bruges is more than just a destination – it's an experience that will leave an indelible mark on your soul.

Immersive History and Culture

Step back in time as you wander through Bruges' well-preserved medieval architecture, where every building tells a story of knights, merchants, and artisans who once roamed these streets. From the towering spires of the Belfry to the intricate lace-like facades of the Town Hall, the city's rich history comes alive at every turn. Dive deeper into its cultural heritage by exploring world-class museums, where masterpieces by renowned Flemish painters await to mesmerize you with their beauty and craftsmanship.

Quaint Canals and Tranquil Beauty

Bruges is often dubbed the "Venice of the North" for good reason – its picturesque canals wind their way through the city, offering a peaceful respite from the hustle and bustle of modern life. Hop aboard a boat tour and drift along the tranquil waters, passing under arched bridges and past charming waterfront homes. Lose yourself in the serenity of the Beguinage courtyard or find solace amidst the lush greenery of the Minnewater Park – in Bruges, nature and history intertwine to create a truly magical experience.

Culinary Adventures

Prepare your taste buds for a culinary journey like no other as you indulge in Bruges' gastronomic delights. From velvety Belgian chocolates to crispy golden waffles, the city's food scene is a feast for the senses. Savor the rich flavors of traditional Flemish cuisine at cozy bistros and taverns, where hearty stews and succulent meats are served with a side of warm hospitality. And let's not forget about the beer – with over 1,000 varieties to choose from, Bruges is a paradise for beer enthusiasts looking to sample the finest brews Belgium has to offer.

Festivals and Cultural Events

Throughout the year, Bruges comes alive with a vibrant array of festivals, concerts, and cultural events that showcase the city's lively spirit. From the colorful spectacle of the Bruges Beer Festival to the melodious strains of the Concertgebouw Brugge, there's always something exciting happening in this dynamic city. Immerse yourself in the local culture by joining in the festivities, where you'll mingle with friendly locals and fellow travelers alike, creating memories that will last a lifetime.

A Sense of Serenity and Solitude

Despite its popularity as a tourist destination, Bruges retains a sense of tranquility and solitude that is both rare and precious. Whether you're wandering through its quiet cobblestone streets or sitting by the canal watching the sunset, you'll find moments of peace and reflection that rejuvenate the soul. In Bruges, time seems to slow down, allowing you to fully immerse yourself in the beauty and wonder of the present moment. Bruges is not just another city – it's a destination like no other, where its history and culture create an unforgettable experience.

WHAT TO EXPECT FROM THIS GUIDE

Welcome to the Bruges Comprehensive Guide, your passport to the enchanting city of Bruges, Belgium. As an author with a plethora of travel guides under my belt, I am thrilled to provide you with an extensive and comprehensive resource to make your journey to Bruges an unforgettable experience. From its medieval charm to its vibrant culture and culinary delights, this guide covers everything you need to know to navigate the cobblestone streets and uncover the hidden treasures of this magical city.

Maps and Navigation:

To help you navigate the cobblestone streets and winding canals of Bruges, this guide includes detailed maps and insider tips to ensure you make the most of your visit. From the historic city center to hidden gems off the beaten path, our maps will guide you to all the must-see attractions and essential landmarks, making it easy to explore Bruges at your own pace.

Accommodation Options:

Bruges offers a wide range of accommodation options to suit every budget and preference. Whether you're looking for a luxury hotel overlooking the canal, a cozy bed and breakfast in the historic city center, or a budget-friendly hostel for the backpacker on a shoestring, this guide has you covered. With detailed descriptions, insider recommendations, and booking tips, finding the perfect place to rest your head in Bruges has never been easier.

Transportation:

Getting to Bruges is a breeze, thanks to its convenient location and excellent transportation links. Whether you're arriving by plane, train, or car, this guide provides essential information on all your travel options, including airports, train stations, and major highways. Once you're in the city, navigating Bruges is a breeze with its efficient public transportation system, including buses, trams, and bicycles. Plus, with our insider tips on walking routes and sightseeing tours, you'll be able to explore Bruges like a local.

Top Attractions:

Bruges is home to a wealth of attractions that will delight history buffs, art enthusiasts, and nature lovers alike. From the iconic Belfry of Bruges and the majestic Basilica of the Holy Blood to the tranquil Minnewater Park and the charming Beguinage, there's no shortage of sights to see and experiences to enjoy in this captivating city. Our guide highlights all the top attractions and hidden gems, along with insider tips and recommendations to help you make the most of your visit.

Practical Information and Travel Resources:

In addition to sightseeing and accommodation, this guide also provides practical information and travel resources to ensure a smooth and hassle-free visit to Bruges. From currency exchange and language tips to safety advice and emergency contacts, we've got you covered with everything you need to know before you go. Plus, with our curated list of recommended travel resources, including websites, apps, and local guides, planning your trip to Bruges has never been easier.

Culinary Delights:

No visit to Bruges would be complete without sampling its culinary delights. From traditional Flemish dishes like stoofvlees and waterzooi to mouthwatering Belgian chocolates and crispy golden waffles, Bruges is a foodie paradise waiting to be explored. Our guide features insider recommendations for the best restaurants, cafes, and food markets in the city, along with tips for navigating the local dining scene like a pro.

Culture and Heritage:

Bruges is steeped in history and culture, with a rich tapestry of art, music, and traditions waiting to be discovered. Explore world-class museums showcasing masterpieces by Flemish painters, attend concerts and performances at historic venues, and immerse yourself in local festivals and celebrations that bring the city to life throughout the year. Our guide provides insight into Bruges' cultural heritage, along with recommendations for cultural experiences that shouldn't be missed.

Outdoor Activities and Adventures:

While Bruges is known for its historic charm, it also offers plenty of opportunities for outdoor adventures and recreational activities. From leisurely canal cruises and scenic bike rides to picnics in the park and nature walks along the city's green spaces, there's no shortage of ways to enjoy Bruges' natural beauty. Our guide includes recommendations for outdoor activities and adventures, along with tips for staying active and exploring the great outdoors during your visit.

Shopping:

Take a piece of Bruges home with you by indulging in a spot of shopping during your visit. From artisanal chocolates and lace to unique handicrafts and souvenirs, Bruges offers a wealth of shopping opportunities for travelers looking to bring home a memento of their time in the city. Our guide highlights the best shopping districts and boutiques in Bruges, along with tips for finding the perfect souvenir to commemorate your visit.

Day Trips and Excursions:

While Bruges is undoubtedly the jewel of Belgium, the surrounding region offers plenty of day trip opportunities for adventurous travelers. Explore the picturesque countryside of Flanders, visit nearby cities like Ghent and Antwerp, or embark on a journey to the Belgian coast for a day of sun, sand, and sea. Our guide provides recommendations for day trips and excursions from Bruges, along with tips for planning and logistics to make the most of your time exploring the region.

Entertainment and Nightlife:

When the sun sets, Bruges comes alive with a vibrant nightlife scene that offers something for everyone. From cozy pubs and traditional Belgian beer bars to chic cocktail lounges and live music venues, there's no shortage of options for evening entertainment in the city. Our guide includes recommendations for nightlife hotspots, along with tips for enjoying Bruges after dark safely and responsibly.

The Bruges Comprehensive Guide is your ultimate companion for exploring the enchanting city of Bruges. With detailed information on maps and navigation, accommodation options, transportation, top attractions, practical tips, culinary delights, cultural experiences, outdoor adventures, shopping opportunities, day trips, and nightlife, this guide covers everything you need to know to make the most of your visit to Bruges.

CHAPTER 1

INTRODUCTION TO BRUGES

1.1 Bruges: A Brief History

Bruges, often referred to as the "Venice of the North," is a city steeped in history and charm, with a rich tapestry of stories waiting to be uncovered by eager visitors. Situated in the Flemish region of Belgium, Bruges has been a bustling hub of trade and culture for centuries, shaping its identity as a medieval marvel and a cultural treasure trove.

Medieval Origins and Golden Age

The history of Bruges dates back to the 9th century when it was founded as a fortress settlement on the banks of the Reie River. By the 12th century, Bruges had emerged as a thriving trading port, thanks to its strategic location near the North Sea and its access to inland waterways. It soon became a key player in the burgeoning wool and cloth trade, attracting merchants from across Europe and beyond. The 14th century marked the golden age of Bruges, as the city reached its zenith of prosperity and influence. With the establishment of the Bourse (Stock Exchange) and the creation of the Burgundian court, Bruges became a center of commerce, culture, and diplomacy, attracting artists, scholars, and nobles from all corners of the continent. Its wealth and power were reflected in its stunning architecture, including the iconic Belfry, the Gothic-style Town Hall, and the opulent Guildhalls that lined its bustling squares.

Decline and Resurgence

However, Bruges' golden age was not to last. In the late 15th century, the silting of the Zwin River and the rise of competing ports led to a gradual decline in Bruges' fortunes. The city's once-thriving economy faltered, and its population dwindled as trade routes shifted elsewhere. By the 17th century, Bruges had fallen into a state of decline and obscurity, its once-grand buildings falling into disrepair and its streets echoing with the whispers of a bygone era. Yet, despite its decline, Bruges never lost its allure. In the 19th century, the city experienced a cultural revival as artists, writers, and intellectuals flocked to its picturesque streets in search of inspiration. The romantic allure of Bruges captured the imagination of the world, with poets like Lord Byron and painters like William Turner immortalizing its beauty in their works. This newfound attention sparked a renewed interest in preserving Bruges' historic heritage, leading to efforts to restore its medieval architecture and revitalize its cultural institutions.

Modern-Day Bruges: A Living Museum

Today, Bruges stands as a living museum, where the past and present converge in a harmonious blend of history, culture, and modernity. Its well-preserved medieval architecture, cobblestone streets, and tranquil canals transport visitors back in time to a bygone era, while its vibrant cultural scene and thriving culinary scene offer a glimpse into contemporary Belgian life. Visitors to Bruges can immerse themselves in its rich history by exploring its myriad attractions, from the towering Belfry and the majestic Basilica of the Holy Blood to the world-class museums and art galleries that line its streets. They can stroll along the picturesque canals, dine in cozy cafes, and sample local delicacies like Belgian chocolates, waffles, and beer, all while soaking in the city's timeless charm and enchanting ambiance.

1.2 Geography and Climate

Located in the northwestern corner of Belgium, Bruges is a city of timeless beauty and enchanting landscapes. Its geography is defined by its location in the Flemish region, where it sits on the flat plains of West Flanders, surrounded by picturesque countryside and dotted with tranquil waterways.

Cityscape and Waterways

The city of Bruges is characterized by its well-preserved medieval architecture, with charming cobblestone streets, gabled rooftops, and towering spires that harken back to a bygone era. The historic city center is crisscrossed by a network of canals, earning Bruges the nickname "Venice of the North." These waterways not only add to the city's scenic beauty but also provide a means of transportation and a source of tranquility for both locals and visitors alike.

Surrounding Landscape

Beyond the city limits, Bruges is surrounded by a patchwork of lush green fields, meandering rivers, and quaint villages, creating a bucolic backdrop that is both serene and picturesque. The Belgian countryside is dotted with windmills, farms, and grazing cattle, evoking a sense of rustic charm and tranquility that contrasts with the bustling energy of the city center.

Climate

Bruges enjoys a temperate maritime climate, characterized by mild summers, cool winters, and ample rainfall throughout the year. Summers are generally pleasant, with average temperatures ranging from 18°C to 25°C (64°F to 77°F), making it an ideal time to explore the city's outdoor attractions and enjoy leisurely strolls along the canals. Winters are relatively mild, with temperatures typically hovering around 3°C to 8°C (37°F to 46°F), though occasional cold snaps and light snowfall are not uncommon.

Spring and Autumn

Spring and autumn are perhaps the best times to visit Bruges, as the city comes alive with blooming flowers, vibrant foliage, and mild temperatures. Springtime, in particular, brings a burst of color to the city as tulips, daffodils, and cherry blossoms adorn its parks and gardens. Autumn, on the other hand, offers crisp air, golden leaves, and fewer crowds, making it an ideal time for exploring Bruges' cultural attractions and outdoor spaces.

Rainfall and Weather Patterns

Rainfall is distributed fairly evenly throughout the year in Bruges, with the wettest months typically occurring in the late summer and early autumn. Visitors should come prepared for occasional showers and overcast skies, especially during the shoulder seasons. However, rain showers in Bruges often pass quickly, giving way to clear skies and sunshine, so don't let a little rain dampen your spirits – there's still plenty to see and do in this enchanting city.

Dressing for the Weather

When packing for your trip to Bruges, it's important to dress appropriately for the weather. In the summer, lightweight clothing, sunscreen, and a hat are essential for staying cool and comfortable in the sun. In the winter, be sure to bundle up with layers, a warm coat, hat, scarf, and gloves to ward off the chill.

And regardless of the season, don't forget to pack a sturdy pair of walking shoes – you'll be doing a lot of exploring on foot in Bruges!

1.3 Getting to Bruges

Embarking on a journey to Bruges is the first step towards immersing yourself in the timeless charm and enchanting beauty of this medieval city. As an author of travel guides and a seasoned explorer, I understand the importance of seamless travel logistics, which is why I'm here to guide you through the various transportation options available for reaching Bruges.

By Air Travel:

For travelers coming from afar, flying into Bruges is often the most convenient option. The closest airport to Bruges is Brussels Airport (BRU), located approximately 100 kilometers away. Brussels Airport serves as a major international hub, with direct flights from cities around the world. Several airlines operate flights to Brussels Airport, including major carriers such as Brussels Airlines, Lufthansa, British Airways, and Air France. Additionally, budget airlines like Ryanair and EasyJet offer affordable options for travelers on a budget. Ticket prices vary depending on factors such as the time of booking, the airline, and the season of travel. Generally, booking in advance and being flexible with your travel dates can help you secure the best deals. Websites like Skyscanner, Expedia, and Google Flights allow you to compare prices from different airlines and book your tickets online with ease. Upon arriving at Brussels Airport, travelers have several options for reaching Bruges. The most convenient and efficient way is by taking a train directly from the airport to Bruges' central station, which typically takes around one hour and offers frequent departures throughout the day. Alternatively, taxis, shuttle services, and rental cars are also available for those who prefer a more personalized mode of transportation.

By Train:

For travelers already in Europe, taking the train to Bruges is a scenic and efficient option. Belgium's extensive rail network connects Bruges to major cities such as Brussels, Ghent, and Antwerp, as well as international destinations like Paris, Amsterdam, and London via high-speed trains. The Belgian National Railway Company (SNCB/NMBS) operates regular train services to Bruges from major cities across Belgium, with direct connections available from Brussels, Antwerp, and Ghent. The journey from Brussels to Bruges typically takes around one hour, offering travelers a comfortable and convenient way to reach their destination. Ticket prices for train travel vary depending on factors such as the class of travel, the type of ticket (flexible or non-flexible), and the time of booking. Discounts are often available for advance purchases, youth travelers, and seniors. Tickets can be purchased online through the SNCB/NMBS website or at train stations throughout Belgium.

By Road:

For travelers who prefer the flexibility and freedom of driving, reaching Bruges by road is a viable option. Belgium's well-maintained road network makes driving to Bruges a relatively straightforward and enjoyable experience, especially for those exploring the surrounding countryside. Bruges is easily accessible by car via major highways such as the E40 and E403, which connect the city to nearby cities like Brussels, Ghent, and Antwerp, as well as international destinations like Amsterdam and Paris. The journey by car from Brussels to Bruges takes approximately one hour, depending on traffic conditions. Travelers driving to Bruges should be aware of factors such as tolls, parking availability, and traffic regulations. Parking facilities are available throughout the city, including metered street parking and public parking garages. Additionally, car rental companies operate at Brussels Airport and in major cities, offering travelers the flexibility to explore Bruges and its surroundings at their own pace. Reaching Bruges is a seamless and straightforward process, thanks to its excellent transportation connections and proximity to major cities and airports. Whether you choose to fly into Brussels Airport, hop on a train from nearby cities, or hit the road and drive to Bruges, rest assured that your journey will be as smooth as possible, allowing you to focus on experiencing all that this magical city has to offer.

1.4 Best Time to Visit

Determining the ideal time to visit Bruges is key to experiencing the city's charm and allure to the fullest. As an author of travel guides and a seasoned traveler, I understand the importance of timing when it comes to planning your visit to this enchanting medieval city. Let's explore the factors that influence the best time to visit Bruges and help you make the most of your trip.

Seasonal Considerations:

Bruges experiences four distinct seasons throughout the year, each offering its own unique charms and attractions. Spring (March to May) brings blooming flowers, mild temperatures, and vibrant foliage, making it an ideal time for exploring the city's parks, gardens, and outdoor attractions. Summer (June to August) sees warmer weather, longer days, and bustling streets filled with tourists and locals alike enjoying outdoor festivals, boat rides along the canals, and al fresco dining in the city's charming squares. Autumn (September to November) brings crisp air, golden leaves, and fewer crowds, making it a perfect time for leisurely walks through Bruges' historic streets and cultural attractions. Winter (December to February) brings chilly temperatures, festive decorations, and the magical atmosphere of the holiday season, with Christmas markets, ice skating rinks, and cozy cafes offering respite from the cold.

Weather Considerations:

Bruges enjoys a temperate maritime climate, characterized by mild summers, cool winters, and ample rainfall throughout the year. While summer offers the most favorable weather for outdoor activities and sightseeing, it also tends to be the busiest and most expensive time to visit Bruges. Spring and autumn offer pleasant temperatures, fewer crowds, and lower prices, making them ideal times for budget-conscious travelers looking to avoid the peak tourist season. Winter may be chilly, but it also brings the festive atmosphere of Christmas markets, holiday lights, and cozy cafes serving warm Belgian chocolates and mulled wine.

Event Considerations:

In addition to seasonal considerations, timing your visit to Bruges to coincide with special events and festivals can enhance your experience and provide unique cultural insights. From the colorful Procession of the Holy Blood in May to the festive Christmas markets in December, Bruges hosts a variety of events and celebrations throughout the year that showcase its rich heritage and vibrant cultural scene. Whether you're a music lover, art enthusiast, or foodie, there's sure to be an event in Bruges that piques your interest and adds an extra layer of excitement to your visit.

Crowd Considerations:

While Bruges is a popular tourist destination year-round, the city experiences peak tourist seasons during the summer months, especially in July and August. During this time, the streets can become crowded with visitors, and popular attractions may have long queues and limited availability. If you prefer to avoid the crowds and enjoy a more relaxed experience, consider visiting Bruges during the shoulder seasons of spring and autumn when the weather is still pleasant, but the tourist crowds are thinner.

Personal Preferences:

Ultimately, the best time to visit Bruges depends on your personal preferences, interests, and priorities. Whether you're drawn to the vibrant energy of summer, the colorful foliage of autumn, or the festive atmosphere of winter, there's something for everyone to enjoy in Bruges year-round. Consider what activities and experiences are most important to you, and plan your visit accordingly to make the most of your time in this enchanting medieval city.

CHAPTER 2

ACCOMMODATION OPTIONS

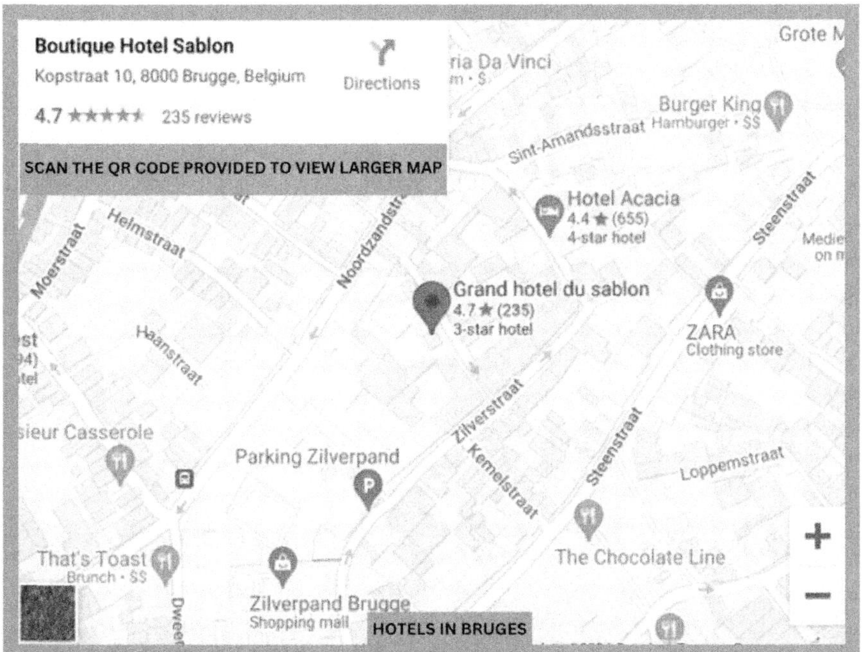

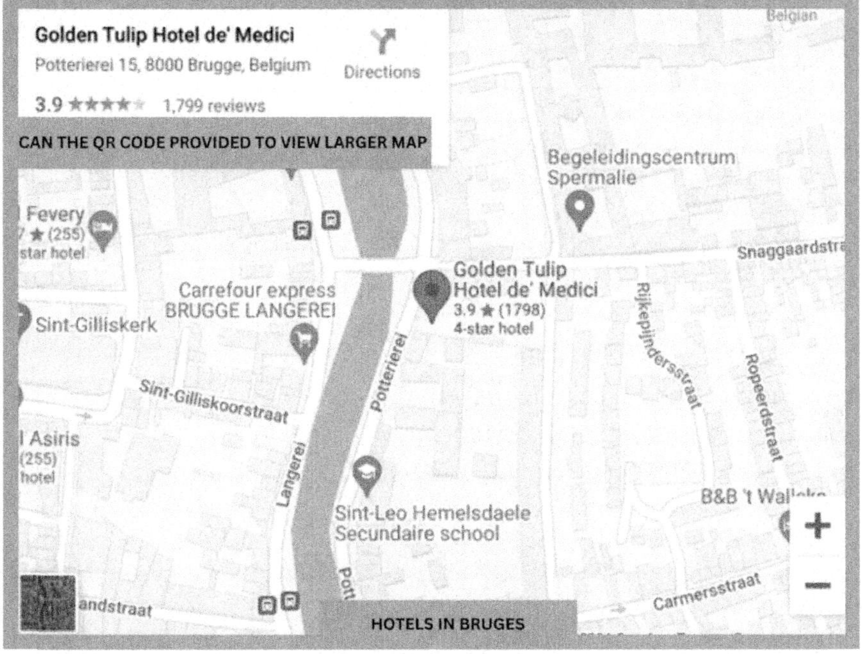

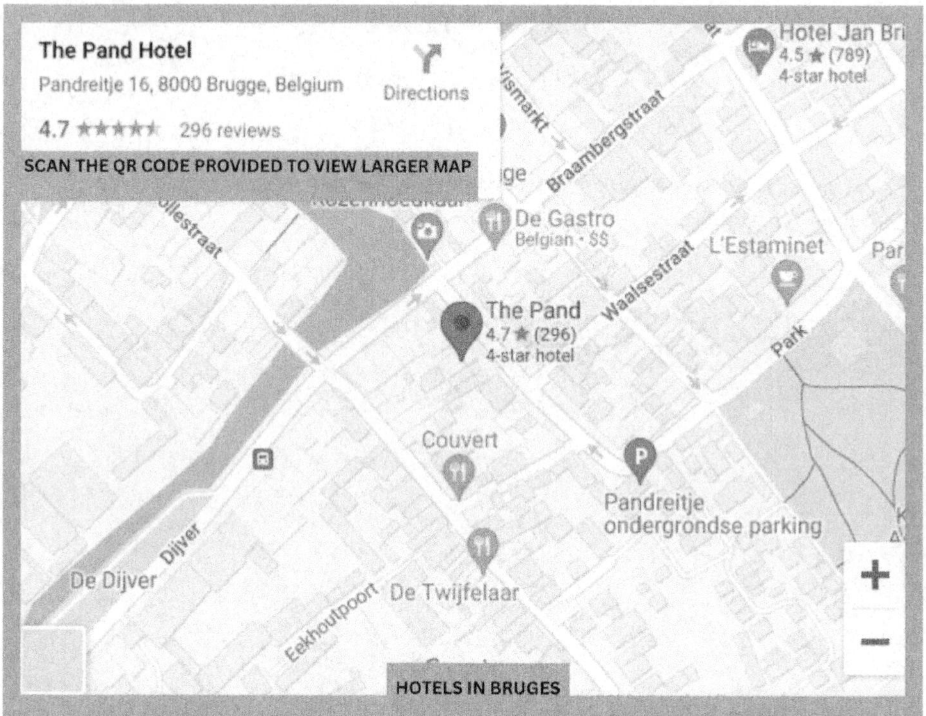

Scan the QR code with a device to view a comprehensive and larger map of various accommodation options in Bruges

HOTELS IN BRUGES

2.1 Hotels and Boutique Inns

As you plan your visit to the enchanting city of Bruges, one of the most important decisions you'll make is where to stay. Fortunately, Bruges offers a wealth of luxurious accommodations, from elegant hotels to charming boutique inns, each offering a unique blend of comfort, style, and hospitality.

Hotel Dukes' Palace Bruges

Nestled within a 15th-century palace in the heart of Bruges, Hotel Dukes' Palace offers a regal retreat for discerning travelers. Located just steps away from the historic city center, this five-star hotel boasts opulent rooms and suites adorned with antique furnishings, plush bedding, and modern amenities. Guests can indulge in gourmet dining at the hotel's Michelin-starred restaurant, relax in the serene courtyard garden, or pamper themselves with a spa treatment at the luxurious wellness center. With its impeccable service and elegant surroundings, Hotel Dukes' Palace Bruges is the epitome of luxury in the heart of Flanders. Website for booking and reservations: https://hoteldukespalace.com/

Relais & Châteaux Hotel Heritage

Situated in a historic 19th-century mansion overlooking Bruges' picturesque canals, Relais & Châteaux Hotel Heritage offers a refined escape from the hustle and bustle of city life. This boutique hotel features individually decorated rooms and suites, each exuding charm and sophistication with period furnishings, marble bathrooms, and modern comforts. Guests can savor exquisite cuisine at the hotel's Michelin-recommended restaurant, unwind in the cozy lounge bar, or take a leisurely stroll through the charming cobblestone streets of Bruges. With its intimate ambiance and personalized service, Relais & Châteaux Hotel Heritage is a hidden gem waiting to be discovered. Website for booking and reservations: https://www.hotel-heritage.com/

Hotel De Orangerie

Tucked away on the banks of Bruges' scenic canals, Hotel De Orangerie offers a tranquil oasis in the heart of the city. Housed within a beautifully restored 15th-century convent, this boutique hotel features elegant rooms and suites with views of the water or the hotel's peaceful garden. Guests can enjoy afternoon tea in the cozy lounge, savor Belgian specialties at the hotel's restaurant, or relax by the fireplace in the library. With its idyllic location and intimate atmosphere, Hotel De Orangerie is the perfect retreat for travelers seeking charm and serenity in Bruges. Website for booking and reservations: https://www.hotelorangerie.be/

Hotel Van Cleef

Set in a historic townhouse in the heart of Bruges' UNESCO-listed city center, Hotel Van Cleef offers a luxurious haven for discerning travelers. Each of the hotel's individually designed rooms and suites reflects a blend of traditional elegance and modern comfort, with antique furnishings, plush bedding, and upscale amenities. Guests can start their day with a gourmet breakfast served in the elegant dining room, unwind in the hotel's private garden, or explore the city's iconic landmarks and attractions just steps away. With its personalized service and attention to detail, Hotel Van Cleef promises a memorable stay in the heart of Bruges. Website for booking and reservations: https://www.hotelvancleef.be/en/

The Pand Hotel

Nestled in a charming 18th-century carriage house in the historic center of Bruges, The Pand Hotel offers a boutique retreat with old-world charm and modern amenities. Each of the hotel's luxurious rooms and suites is individually decorated with elegant fabrics, antique furnishings, and contemporary touches, creating a cozy and inviting ambiance. Guests can relax in the hotel's intimate lounge, enjoy a drink by the fireplace, or venture out to explore the city's cobblestone streets and hidden treasures. With its warm hospitality and attention to detail, The Pand Hotel is a true gem in the heart of Bruges. Website for booking and reservations: https://pandhotel.com/

Hotel Jan Brito

Step back in time and immerse yourself in the rich history of Bruges with a stay at Hotel Jan Brito, a charming boutique hotel located in a historic 16th-century mansion. Nestled in a quiet residential area just a short walk from the city's main attractions, this elegant hotel offers a peaceful retreat away from the hustle and bustle of the city center. The hotel's beautifully appointed rooms and suites feature traditional decor, antique furnishings, and modern amenities, providing guests with a comfortable and inviting atmosphere. Guests can relax in the hotel's picturesque courtyard garden, enjoy a drink at the cozy bar, or explore the nearby shops and restaurants. With its historic ambiance, personalized service, and warm hospitality, Hotel Jan Brito offers a truly memorable experience for travelers seeking a taste of Bruges' timeless charm. Website for booking and reservations: https://www.janbrito.com/en/

2.2 Bed and Breakfasts

As you plan your escape to the picturesque city of Bruges, consider immersing yourself in the warmth and hospitality of a traditional Bed and Breakfast. Bruges boasts a plethora of charming B&Bs, each offering a unique blend of comfort, character, and personalized service.

B&B Huyze Weyne

Nestled in a historic townhouse just a stone's throw away from Bruges' bustling city center, B&B Huyze Weyne offers a tranquil retreat with a touch of old-world charm. Each of the cozy guest rooms is elegantly appointed with antique furnishings, plush bedding, and modern amenities. Guests can start their day with a hearty breakfast served in the quaint dining room, relax in the peaceful garden courtyard, or explore the nearby attractions on foot or by bicycle. With its warm hospitality and convenient location, B&B Huyze Weyne is the perfect home base for exploring the sights and sounds of Bruges. Website for booking and reservations: https://www.huyzeweyne.be/

B&B 't Walleke

Situated in a quiet residential neighborhood just a short walk from Bruges' historic city center, B&B 't Walleke offers a cozy haven away from the hustle and bustle of city life. The charming guest rooms are tastefully decorated with comfortable furnishings, colorful accents, and modern amenities. Guests can enjoy a delicious homemade breakfast served in the sunny breakfast room, unwind in the peaceful garden terrace, or explore the city's hidden gems with the help of the friendly hosts. With its relaxed atmosphere and personalized service, B&B 't Walleke provides a warm welcome to travelers seeking a true home away from home in Bruges. Website for booking and reservations: https://bruggebedandbreakfast.be/

B&B Asinello

Located in a historic building overlooking Bruges' scenic canals, B&B Asinello offers a charming retreat with panoramic views of the city's iconic landmarks. The intimate guest rooms feature elegant décor, comfortable furnishings, and modern amenities, creating a cozy and inviting atmosphere for guests to relax and unwind. Guests can start their day with a sumptuous breakfast served in the elegant dining room, take a leisurely stroll along the canals, or explore the nearby shops and restaurants. With its picturesque location and personalized service, B&B Asinello is the perfect choice for travelers seeking a memorable stay in the heart of Bruges. Website for booking and reservations: https://www.asinello.be/nl/

B&B St. Jacobs

Set in a beautifully restored townhouse in Bruges' historic city center, B&B St. Jacobs offers a peaceful retreat with a touch of luxury. Each of the spacious guest rooms is elegantly furnished with modern comforts, while retaining the charm and character of the original building. Guests can enjoy a delicious breakfast served in the cozy dining room, relax in the private garden courtyard, or explore the city's cultural attractions with ease. With its central location and warm hospitality, B&B St. Jacobs provides a welcoming haven for travelers seeking comfort and convenience in Bruges. Website for booking and reservations: https://www.stjacobs.eu/en/

Canal Deluxe Bed & Breakfast

Experience the enchanting beauty of Bruges' iconic canals with a stay at Canal Deluxe Bed & Breakfast, a charming waterfront retreat located in the heart of the city's historic center. This elegant bed and breakfast offers luxurious accommodations with stunning views of the canal, providing guests with a serene and picturesque setting for their stay in Bruges. Each of the beautifully appointed guest rooms features plush bedding, antique furnishings, and modern amenities, ensuring a comfortable and memorable experience. Guests can enjoy a delicious breakfast served each morning in the elegant dining room, as well as complimentary Wi-Fi and personalized concierge services to enhance their stay. With its prime location, luxurious accommodations, and warm hospitality, Canal Deluxe Bed & Breakfast provides a truly unforgettable experience for travelers visiting Bruges. Website for booking and reservations: https://www.canaldeluxe.com/

B&B Number 11 Exclusive Guesthouse

Situated in a historic mansion in the heart of Bruges' UNESCO-listed city center, B&B Number 11 Exclusive Guesthouse offers a luxurious retreat with modern amenities and personalized service. The elegantly appointed guest rooms feature stylish décor, plush bedding, and upscale amenities, ensuring a comfortable and memorable stay for guests. Guests can indulge in a gourmet breakfast served in the elegant dining room, relax in the tranquil garden terrace, or explore the city's iconic landmarks and attractions just steps away. With its intimate atmosphere and attention to detail, B&B Number 11 Exclusive Guesthouse offers a truly unforgettable experience in Bruges. Website for booking and reservations: https://www.number11.be/en/

2.3 Vacation Rentals and Apartments

As you embark on your journey to the captivating city of Bruges, consider immersing yourself in the local culture and lifestyle by staying in a vacation rental or apartment. Bruges offers a variety of charming accommodations, from historic apartments to modern lofts, each providing a unique opportunity to experience the city like a local.

B&B Casa Romantico

Located in a quiet residential neighborhood just a short walk from Bruges' historic city center, B&B Casa Romantico offers a charming vacation rental with modern amenities and personalized service. The cozy apartment features a comfortable bedroom, spacious living area, and fully equipped kitchenette, providing guests with all the comforts of home during their stay. Guests can enjoy complimentary breakfast served in the privacy of their apartment, as well as access to the shared garden terrace. With its intimate atmosphere and attentive hosts, B&B Casa Romantico is the perfect retreat for couples seeking a romantic getaway in Bruges. Website for booking and reservations: https://www.casa-romantico.be/nl/

Dukes Arches

Set in a historic building in the heart of Bruges' city center, Dukes Arches offers a luxurious vacation rental with modern amenities and elegant décor. The spacious apartment features a fully equipped kitchen, comfortable living area, and stylish furnishings, providing guests with a comfortable and stylish retreat during their stay. Guests can enjoy complimentary Wi-Fi, flat-screen TVs, and a welcome basket upon arrival, as well as personalized recommendations and assistance from the friendly hosts. With its central location and upscale amenities, Dukes Arches is the perfect choice for travelers seeking a luxurious and convenient stay in Bruges. Website for booking and reservations: https://www.dukesarches.com/

Guesthouse 17

Nestled in a historic townhouse in Bruges' picturesque city center, Guesthouse 17 offers a charming vacation rental with modern amenities and personalized service. The cozy apartment features a fully equipped kitchen, comfortable living area, and private terrace, providing guests with a peaceful retreat after a day of exploring the city. Guests can enjoy complimentary breakfast served in the privacy of their apartment, as well as access to the shared garden courtyard. With its warm hospitality and convenient location, Guesthouse 17 is the perfect home away from home for travelers seeking a memorable stay in Bruges. Website for booking and reservations: https://www.pand17.com/en/

Breydelhof Apartments

Escape the hustle and bustle of the city with a stay at Breydelhof Apartments, a tranquil oasis located just outside the historic center of Bruges. Surrounded by lush greenery and scenic views, these spacious apartments offer a peaceful retreat for guests looking to unwind and recharge. Each apartment features a fully equipped kitchen, comfortable living area, and private terrace or balcony, providing guests with all the comforts of home during their stay. Guests can also enjoy access to a communal garden, barbecue facilities, and complimentary bicycles for exploring the picturesque countryside. With its serene ambiance and idyllic setting, Breydelhof Apartments offers a unique and relaxing experience for travelers visiting Bruges. Website for booking and reservations: https://www.breydelhof.be/

2.4 Hostels and Budget Accommodations

As you plan your visit to the charming city of Bruges, finding budget-friendly accommodations that don't compromise on comfort and convenience is essential. Bruges offers a variety of hostels and budget accommodations, providing travelers with a comfortable and affordable place to stay while exploring the city's historic streets and picturesque canals.

Bruges Hostel

Located just a short walk from Bruges' historic city center, Bruges Hostel offers budget-friendly accommodations in a vibrant and sociable atmosphere. The hostel features dormitory-style rooms with bunk beds, as well as private rooms for those seeking a bit more privacy. Guests can enjoy complimentary Wi-Fi, a fully equipped kitchen for self-catering, and a cozy lounge area for relaxing and socializing with fellow travelers. With its central location and affordable rates, Bruges Hostel is the perfect choice for backpackers and budget-conscious travelers looking to explore the city on a budget. Website for booking and reservations: https://www.hostelz.com/hostels/Belgium/Bruges

Lybeer Travellers' Hostel

Situated in a historic building in the heart of Bruges' city center, Lybeer Travellers' Hostel offers budget-friendly accommodations with a cozy and welcoming atmosphere. The hostel features dormitory-style rooms with comfortable beds and individual lockers, as well as private rooms for couples or small groups. Guests can take advantage of the hostel's communal kitchen, lounge area, and outdoor terrace, as well as complimentary Wi-Fi throughout the property. With its central location and friendly staff, Lybeer Travellers' Hostel provides a convenient and affordable base for exploring the sights and sounds of Bruges. Website for booking and reservations: http://www.hostellybeer.com/

St. Christopher's Inn Hostel

Located just steps away from Bruges' iconic Belfry Tower, St. Christopher's Inn Hostel offers budget-friendly accommodations with a lively and social atmosphere. The hostel features dormitory-style rooms with comfortable beds, individual lockers, and ensuite bathrooms, as well as private rooms for couples or small groups. Guests can enjoy a complimentary breakfast served in the hostel's onsite restaurant, as well as discounted drinks and food at the lively bar. With its central location, vibrant atmosphere, and affordable rates, St. Christopher's Inn Hostel is a popular choice for young backpackers and solo travelers visiting Bruges. Website for booking and reservations: https://www.st-christophers.co.uk/bruges/

Snuffel Backpacker Hostel

Nestled in a historic building in Bruges' picturesque city center, Snuffel Backpacker Hostel offers budget-friendly accommodations with a cozy and relaxed vibe. The hostel features dormitory-style rooms with comfortable beds, individual lockers, and shared bathrooms, as well as private rooms for couples or small groups. Guests can enjoy complimentary Wi-Fi, a communal kitchen for self-catering, and a cozy lounge area for socializing with fellow travelers. With its central location and laid-back atmosphere, Snuffel Backpacker Hostel provides a welcoming and affordable option for travelers seeking a true backpacker experience in Bruges. Website for booking and reservations: https://snuffel.be/

Charlie Rockets Youth Hostel

Located in a historic building in the heart of Bruges' city center, Charlie Rockets Youth Hostel offers budget-friendly accommodations with a fun and energetic atmosphere. The hostel features dormitory-style rooms with comfortable beds, individual lockers, and ensuite bathrooms, as well as private rooms for couples or small groups. Guests can enjoy a complimentary breakfast served in the hostel's onsite restaurant, as well as discounted drinks and food at the lively bar. With its central location, vibrant atmosphere, and affordable rates, Charlie Rockets Youth Hostel is a popular choice for young travelers and backpackers visiting Bruges. Website for booking and reservations: https://hotel-charlie-rockets.hotelescuatroestrellas.website/

2.5 Unique Stays in Bruges

As you plan your visit to the charming city of Bruges, why not step off the beaten path and indulge in a truly unique accommodation experience? Bruges offers a variety of one-of-a-kind stays that promise to elevate your trip from ordinary to extraordinary. From historic landmarks to unconventional accommodations, these unique stays offer a blend of charm, comfort, and memorable experiences that will make your visit to Bruges truly unforgettable.

Boat Hotel De Barge

Experience the magic of Bruges' picturesque canals with a stay at Boat Hotel De Barge, a unique floating hotel located in the heart of the city. This charming boat hotel offers comfortable accommodations in cozy cabins, each with its own ensuite bathroom and stunning views of the water. Guests can relax on the sun deck, enjoy a drink in the onboard bar, or take a leisurely cruise along the canals with the friendly captain. With its central location and nautical charm, Boat Hotel De Barge offers a truly unique and unforgettable experience in Bruges. Website for booking and reservations: https://www.hoteldebarge.be/en/

Hotel Ter Brughe

Nestled along the picturesque Dijver Canal in the historic city center of Bruges, Hotel Ter Brughe offers a unique blend of medieval charm and modern comfort. This former 15th-century monastery has been lovingly restored into a boutique hotel with elegant rooms and suites overlooking the tranquil canal. Guests can relax in the peaceful courtyard garden, enjoy a drink in the cozy lounge bar, or explore the city's iconic landmarks and attractions just steps away. With its historic ambiance and prime location, Hotel Ter Brughe offers a truly unique and immersive experience in the heart of Bruges. Website for booking and reservations: https://www.hotelterbrughe.com/

B&B Bariseele

Situated in a historic townhouse just a short walk from Bruges' bustling city center, B&B Bariseele offers a unique blend of elegance and comfort in a tranquil setting. This charming bed and breakfast features beautifully appointed rooms and suites with luxurious amenities, including plush bedding, marble bathrooms, and antique furnishings. Guests can enjoy a gourmet breakfast served in the elegant dining room, relax in the peaceful garden courtyard, or explore the nearby shops and attractions. With its personalized service and intimate atmosphere, B&B Bariseele provides a unique and memorable stay in Bruges. Website for booking and reservations: https://www.bariseele.be/

Hotel Navarra Bruges

Situated in a historic 17th-century building in the heart of Bruges' city center, Hotel Navarra Bruges offers a unique blend of old-world charm and modern luxury. This elegant hotel features beautifully appointed rooms and suites, each decorated with classic Belgian flair and equipped with modern amenities for a comfortable stay. Guests can relax in the hotel's tranquil courtyard garden, unwind in the indoor swimming pool and sauna, or enjoy a drink at the stylish bar. With its central location and timeless elegance, Hotel Navarra Bruges provides a truly unique and memorable experience for discerning travelers. Website for booking and reservations: https://www.hotelnavarra.com/

La Maison Bruges

Experience the epitome of luxury and refinement at La Maison Bruges, a stunning boutique hotel housed within a meticulously restored 17th-century mansion in the heart of Bruges' historic city center. Each of the hotel's lavish suites is elegantly appointed with bespoke furnishings, plush bedding, and modern amenities, offering guests the ultimate in comfort and indulgence. Guests can savor gourmet breakfasts served in the elegant dining room, unwind in the private garden terrace, or enjoy personalized concierge services to enhance their stay. With its unparalleled elegance and sophistication, La Maison Bruges offers a truly unique and unforgettable retreat in the heart of Bruges. Website for booking and reservations: https://www.maisonbruges.com/

CHAPTER 3

TRANSPORTATION IN BRUGES

3.1 Public Transportation

Exploring the picturesque city of Bruges, Belgium, is made effortlessly convenient through its well-structured public transportation system, catering to both locals and tourists alike. Known for its well-preserved medieval architecture and charming canals, Bruges offers an array of transportation options to navigate its cobblestone streets and historic landmarks. Bruges boasts a comprehensive public transportation network comprising buses, trams, and boats, ensuring seamless connectivity throughout the city and its outskirts. The primary modes of transportation include the De Lijn buses, which operate within the city and link it to neighboring areas, and the De Lijn trams, offering efficient travel to nearby towns like Blankenberge and Knokke.

De Lijn Buses

De Lijn buses serve as the backbone of Bruges' public transit system, providing extensive coverage across the city and its surrounding regions. These buses are equipped with modern amenities and adhere to punctual schedules, ensuring reliable transportation for commuters and visitors alike. The fare for a single journey on a De Lijn bus typically ranges from €2 to €3, depending on the distance traveled. However, travelers can opt for money-saving options such as day passes or multi-day passes, offering unlimited rides within specified time frames.

De Lijn Trams

For those looking to venture beyond the city limits, De Lijn trams offer a convenient mode of transportation to explore the coastal towns near Bruges. Trams connect Bruges to popular destinations like Blankenberge and Knokke, allowing passengers to enjoy scenic journeys along the Belgian coastline. Similar to bus fares, the cost of a tram ticket varies based on the distance traveled, with options for day passes and multi-day passes available for frequent travelers.

Boat Tours

In addition to conventional land-based transportation, Bruges also offers enchanting boat tours along its iconic canals, providing a unique perspective of the city's architectural marvels and historic landmarks. These leisurely boat rides offer a tranquil escape from the bustling streets, allowing passengers to soak in the beauty of Bruges' picturesque waterways. While boat tours may not serve as primary means of transportation, they offer an unparalleled experience for tourists seeking to immerse themselves in the city's rich heritage.

Navigating Bruges Effectively

Navigating Bruges' public transportation system effectively requires careful planning and familiarity with the city's routes and schedules. To optimize travel experiences, visitors can utilize various resources such as route maps, online journey planners, and mobile applications offered by De Lijn. These tools provide real-time information on bus and tram schedules, helping travelers plan their itineraries and minimize waiting times. Furthermore, tourists can benefit from tourist information centers located throughout the city, where knowledgeable staff members can offer assistance with route planning, ticket purchases, and general inquiries about Bruges' public transportation network. Additionally, many hotels and accommodations in Bruges provide guests with complimentary city maps and transportation guides, facilitating seamless exploration of the city's attractions.

3.2 Walking and Cycling in Bruges

Bruges, often called "Venice of the North," is a city rich in history and adorned with architectural marvels, making it a delight to explore on foot or by bicycle. With its well-preserved medieval streets, charming squares, and tranquil canals, Bruges offers visitors an enchanting experience, whether strolling leisurely or pedaling through its picturesque landscapes.

Walking in Bruges:

One of the most delightful ways to immerse oneself in the beauty of Bruges is by embarking on a leisurely walk through its cobblestone streets and labyrinthine alleys. The city's compact size and pedestrian-friendly infrastructure make it an ideal destination for exploring on foot, allowing visitors to discover hidden gems at every turn. From the iconic Markt square with its towering Belfry to the serene Beguinage with its whitewashed houses, Bruges beckons walkers to unravel its rich tapestry of history and culture. As one meanders through Bruges, they will encounter a myriad of architectural wonders, including medieval churches, Gothic facades, and quaint bridges spanning the city's picturesque canals. Along the way, charming cafes, artisanal boutiques, and bustling market stalls offer opportunities to indulge in local delicacies and artisanal crafts, adding to the sensory experience of exploring Bruges on foot.

Cycling:

In addition to walking, cycling is a popular mode of transportation and recreation in Bruges, reflecting Belgium's rich cycling culture. The city boasts an extensive network of bike paths and dedicated lanes, making it easy and safe for cyclists to navigate its streets and outskirts. Visitors can rent bicycles from various rental shops located throughout the city, with options ranging from traditional bikes to electric bicycles for those seeking a more leisurely ride.

Cycling in Bruges offers a unique perspective of the city's enchanting landscapes, allowing riders to venture beyond the beaten path and explore its verdant parks, tranquil canals, and scenic countryside. From the lush greenery of Minnewater Park to the serene shores of the Damme Canal, cyclists can escape the hustle and bustle of the city center and embrace the natural beauty that surrounds Bruges.

Practical Considerations for Walking and Cycling

While exploring Bruges on foot or by bike is a rewarding experience, there are practical considerations to keep in mind to ensure a smooth and enjoyable journey. Visitors should familiarize themselves with the city's traffic rules and regulations, particularly when cycling, to ensure safety on the roads and pedestrian paths. Additionally, wearing comfortable footwear and clothing suitable for walking or cycling is essential, especially during inclement weather. Visitors may also consider bringing along a map or using navigation apps to help navigate the city's streets and landmarks effectively.

3.3 Taxi and Ridesharing Services

In addition to its extensive public transportation network and pedestrian-friendly infrastructure, Bruges offers visitors the convenience of taxis and ride-sharing services, providing efficient and comfortable options for getting around the city and its environs. Whether traveling to a specific destination or exploring the city at leisure, taxis and ride-sharing services offer flexibility and convenience to suit diverse travel needs.

Taxis:

Taxis are a familiar sight on the streets of Bruges, offering a convenient mode of transportation for those seeking direct and personalized service. Visitors can easily hail taxis from designated taxi stands located throughout the city center or book them through local taxi companies via phone or mobile applications. Taxis in Bruges typically operate on metered fares, with rates based on distance traveled and waiting time. While taxi fares may vary slightly among different operators, passengers can expect transparent pricing and reliable service from licensed taxi drivers.

Ride-Sharing Services:

In recent years, ride-sharing services have gained popularity in Bruges, providing travelers with an alternative to traditional taxis and public transportation. Platforms such as Uber (https://www.uber.com/) and Lyft (https://www.lyft.com/) offer convenient and cost-effective options for getting around the city, allowing passengers to request rides with ease through their smartphone apps. Ride-sharing services in Bruges operate on dynamic pricing models, with fares determined by factors such as distance, demand, and time of day. While ride-sharing may offer competitive pricing compared to taxis, passengers should be mindful of surge pricing during peak hours or special events.

Accessing Taxis and Ride-Sharing Services

Accessing taxis and ride-sharing services in Bruges is straightforward, thanks to the city's well-developed infrastructure and digital connectivity. Visitors can download mobile applications for popular ride-sharing platforms such as Uber or Lyft and create accounts to request rides within minutes. Additionally, taxi stands are strategically located in high-traffic areas, including train stations, major squares, and tourist attractions, making it easy for passengers to hail taxis on the go. For those preferring the convenience of pre-booked rides, many local taxi companies offer online booking services through their websites or dedicated mobile apps.

Considerations for Using Taxis and Ride-Sharing Services

While taxis and ride-sharing services offer convenient options for getting around Bruges, there are certain considerations to keep in mind to ensure a smooth and enjoyable experience. Passengers should always verify the legitimacy of taxi operators and ride-sharing drivers to ensure safety and reliability. Additionally, travelers should familiarize themselves with local regulations and etiquette when using taxis, including tipping practices and standard fare rates. Furthermore, passengers should exercise caution when sharing personal information or payment details through ride-sharing apps and adhere to safety guidelines provided by the service providers. By exercising common sense and awareness, visitors can enjoy the convenience and comfort of taxis and ride-sharing services while exploring the enchanting city of Bruges.

3.4 Car Rentals and Driving Tips

For travelers seeking the ultimate flexibility and independence in exploring Bruges and its surrounding areas, car rentals provide the perfect solution. With a plethora of rental companies offering a wide range of vehicles, visitors can embark on memorable road trips, uncover hidden gems, and navigate the Belgian countryside at their own pace.

Car Rental Companies in Bruges:

Several reputable car rental companies operate in Bruges, catering to the diverse needs and preferences of travelers. Names such as Europcar (https://www.europcar.com/), Avis (https://www.avis.com/), Hertz (https://www.hertz.com/rentacar/), and Sixt (https://www.sixt.com/) are among the well-known rental providers offering a variety of vehicles ranging from compact cars to spacious vans and SUVs. These companies have rental offices conveniently located at Bruges' main train station, airport, and city center, providing easy access for visitors arriving by different modes of transportation.

Prices and Booking Procedures

Car rental prices in Bruges vary depending on factors such as vehicle type, rental duration, and insurance coverage. Generally, rates are competitive and can be tailored to suit individual budgets and preferences. Visitors can compare prices and book rentals through the companies' official websites or third-party booking platforms. Additionally, booking in advance often yields discounts and special offers, ensuring cost-effective transportation solutions for travelers.

Accessing Car Rentals

Accessing car rental services in Bruges is convenient, with rental offices located strategically in key areas of the city. Visitors arriving at Bruges' train station or airport can easily access rental counters within the terminal buildings, where friendly staff members assist with the rental process and vehicle selection. For those staying in the city center, many car rental companies offer delivery and pickup services, allowing customers to have their chosen vehicle brought directly to their accommodation.

Driving Tips for Bruges

Navigating Bruges and its environs by car offers unparalleled freedom and flexibility, but it's essential to familiarize oneself with local driving regulations and etiquette to ensure a safe and enjoyable experience. Here are some key driving tips for exploring Bruges:

Traffic Rules: Familiarize yourself with Belgian traffic rules, including speed limits, right-of-way, and parking regulations. Pay attention to road signs and markings to avoid traffic violations.

City Center Restrictions: Certain areas of Bruges' historic city center are pedestrian-only zones or have restricted vehicle access. Be mindful of signage indicating these zones and adhere to regulations to avoid fines.

Parking: Utilize designated parking areas and garages when exploring Bruges by car. On-street parking may be limited and subject to time restrictions and fees.

Canal Bridges: Exercise caution when crossing canal bridges, as they are often narrow and may require yielding to oncoming traffic. Be patient and courteous to other drivers to ensure smooth traffic flow.

Bicycle Awareness: Bruges is a bike-friendly city, with cyclists sharing the road with motor vehicles. Give cyclists ample space and respect their right of way to ensure safety for all road users.

By adhering to these driving tips and exercising caution on the road, visitors can enjoy the freedom and convenience of exploring Bruges by car while respecting local traffic regulations and promoting safety for themselves and others.

3.5 Boat Tours and Canal Cruises

Immerse yourself in the enchanting beauty of Bruges by embarking on a boat tour or canal cruise, offering a unique perspective of this picturesque Belgian city. With its intricate network of canals winding through historic neighborhoods and under charming bridges, Bruges reveals its timeless allure from the tranquil waters below.

Tranquil Waterways:

Step aboard a traditional canal boat and leave the hustle and bustle of the city behind as you glide gently along Bruges' tranquil waterways. The rhythmic lapping of the water against the boat's hull sets a soothing backdrop for your journey, inviting you to unwind and savor the beauty of your surroundings. As you drift past centuries-old buildings adorned with ivy-clad facades and colorful flower boxes, you'll feel transported to a bygone era of elegance and charm.

Historical Narratives:

As your knowledgeable guide narrates the history of Bruges and its iconic landmarks, you'll gain fascinating insights into the city's past and present. Learn about the medieval merchants who once plied these waterways, trading goods from distant lands and contributing to Bruges' prosperity as a thriving trading hub. Hear tales of romance and intrigue as you pass beneath the iconic Lover's Bridge, where lovers traditionally affix padlocks as tokens of their affection.

Architectural Marvels:

From the vantage point of your boat, you'll have the opportunity to admire Bruges' architectural marvels from a unique angle. Marvel at the intricate Gothic spires of the Church of Our Lady, the grandeur of the Belfry towering over the Markt square, and the graceful curves of the historic stone bridges that span the city's waterways. Each building tells a story of Bruges' illustrious past, reflecting the city's status as a cultural and artistic treasure trove.

Seasonal Splendor:

Depending on the time of year, your boat tour may offer glimpses of Bruges adorned in seasonal splendor. In spring, vibrant blooms line the canal banks, infusing the city with a riot of color and fragrance. Summer brings lazy afternoons basking in the warm sunlight, while autumn paints the landscape in hues of gold and crimson as leaves carpet the water's surface. Even in winter, Bruges exudes a magical charm, with festive decorations adorning the streets and twinkling lights reflecting off the tranquil canals.

Practical Considerations:

To make the most of your boat tour or canal cruise in Bruges, consider these practical tips:

Dress comfortably: Be prepared for varying weather conditions and dress in layers to stay comfortable throughout your tour.

Arrive early: Boat tours can be popular, especially during peak tourist season, so arrive early to secure your spot and avoid long wait times.

Bring a camera: Capture the beauty of Bruges from the water with your camera or smartphone, but don't forget to put it down occasionally and simply soak in the experience with your own eyes.

CHAPTER 4

TOP ATTRACTIONS AND HIDDEN GEMS

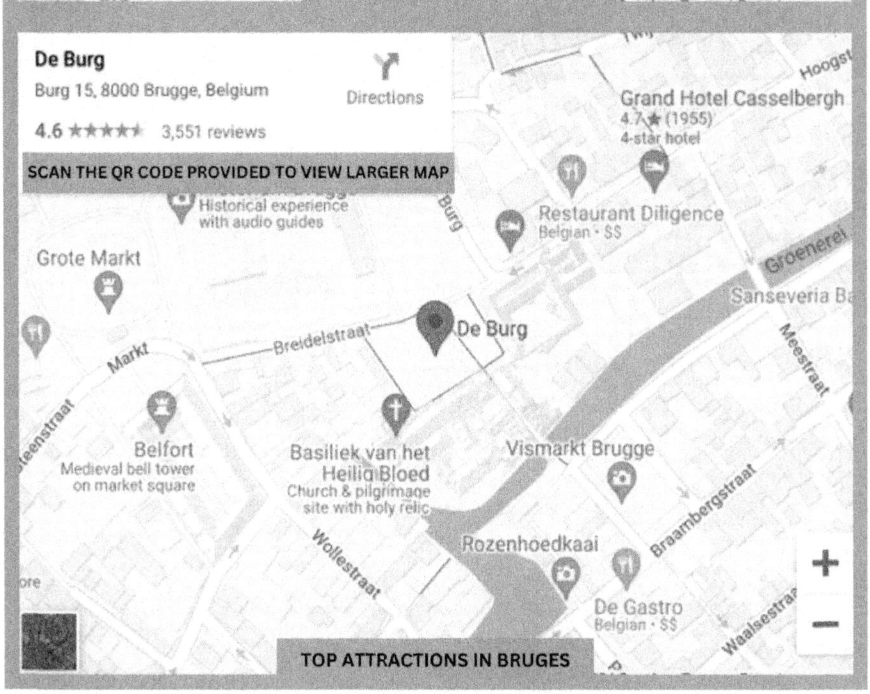

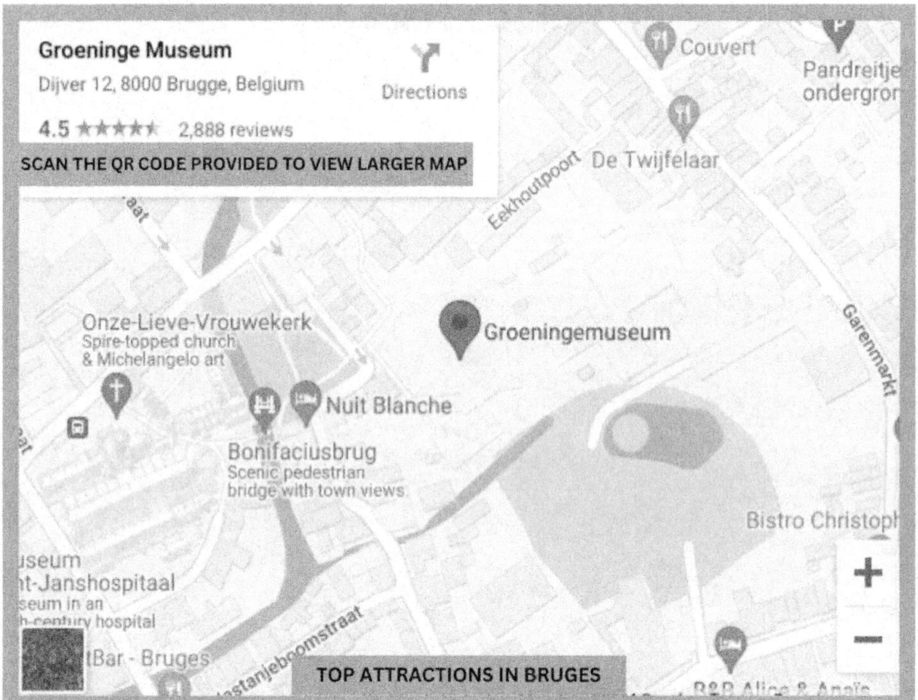

Scan the QR Code with a device to view a comprehensive and larger map of Top Attractions in Bruges

TOP ATTRACTIONS IN BRUGES

4.1 Belfry of Bruges

Located within the charming medieval city of Bruges, Belgium, the Belfry of Bruges stands tall and proud, casting its shadow over the picturesque landscape. This iconic landmark has captivated visitors for centuries, drawing them in with its rich history, architectural splendor, and breathtaking panoramic views.

Location and Accessibility

Situated in the heart of Bruges' historic center, the Belfry rises prominently from the Markt Square, a bustling hub teeming with lively markets, quaint cafes, and centuries-old buildings. Its central location makes it easily accessible by foot from various points within the city. For those traveling from farther afield, Bruges is well-connected by train, with the central station just a short distance from the city center. Additionally, bus services and guided tours offer convenient options for reaching Bruges from neighboring cities such as Brussels and Ghent.

Entry Fee and Practical Information

Unlike some attractions that require hefty admission fees, the Belfry of Bruges offers visitors the opportunity to ascend its towering heights for a modest fee, making it accessible to travelers of all budgets. Upon arrival, visitors can purchase tickets at the base of the tower, with discounts often available for students, seniors, and families. It's worth noting that while the climb to the top may be challenging for some, the experience and views awaiting at the summit make it well worth the effort.

Historical and Cultural Significance

The Belfry of Bruges stands as a testament to the city's rich medieval heritage and its status as a prominent trading center during the Middle Ages. Originally constructed in the 13th century, the tower served as both a symbol of municipal power and a practical means of communication, with its bells ringing out to signal important events and emergencies. Over the centuries, the Belfry has weathered wars, fires, and renovations, yet it remains a beloved emblem of Bruges' enduring resilience and architectural prowess.

Why Visit?

Visiting the Belfry of Bruges offers a multifaceted experience that appeals to history buffs, architecture enthusiasts, and avid photographers alike. Ascending the tower's narrow spiral staircase, visitors are transported back in time as they pass centuries-old stone walls and intricate wooden beams. Upon reaching the summit, they are rewarded with unparalleled panoramic views of Bruges and its surrounding countryside, providing a unique vantage point to appreciate the city's beauty and charm.

What to Do

Aside from admiring the Belfry's exterior and ascending its heights, visitors can explore the surrounding Markt Square, immersing themselves in the lively atmosphere of this historic gathering place. Nearby attractions such as the Gothic-style Town Hall and the bustling Belfry Market offer further opportunities for exploration and cultural discovery. Additionally, guided tours and audio guides are available for those seeking a deeper understanding of the Belfry's history and significance.

Practical Tips for Visitors

Before embarking on a journey to the Belfry of Bruges, it's advisable to check opening hours and any temporary closures due to maintenance or special events. Comfortable footwear and suitable clothing are essential for the climb, especially during colder months when temperatures can be brisk at the summit. Additionally, visitors should be mindful of their belongings and respectful of other guests, particularly during peak tourist seasons when crowds may be larger.

4.2 Markt (Market Square)

Nestled at the heart of the enchanting city of Bruges, Belgium, lies Markt, also known as Market Square—a bustling epicenter of activity, culture, and history.

Location and Accessibility

Markt occupies a central position within Bruges' historic city center, making it easily accessible by foot from various points within the city. For those arriving from afar, Bruges is well-connected by train, with the central station situated within walking distance of Markt. Additionally, bus services and guided tours offer convenient transportation options for travelers exploring the region.

Entry Fee and Practical Information

One of the most enticing aspects of Markt is its accessibility to all, as there is no entry fee required to experience the vibrant energy of this historic square.

Visitors are free to wander among the colorful stalls, admire the architectural splendor of surrounding buildings, and soak in the lively atmosphere without any financial barrier. However, it's important to note that additional charges may apply for specific activities or attractions within the square.

Historical and Cultural Significance

Markt holds a storied history that spans centuries, dating back to medieval times when it served as a bustling marketplace and social gathering place for Bruges' residents. Over the years, the square has witnessed the ebb and flow of commerce, the rise and fall of empires, and the enduring spirit of community that defines Bruges' identity. Today, it stands as a living monument to the city's rich heritage and a testament to its resilience in the face of change.

Why Visit?

There are countless reasons why a visit to Markt is an essential part of any trip to Bruges. For history enthusiasts, the square offers a captivating glimpse into the city's medieval past, with its well-preserved architecture and cobblestone streets evoking a sense of bygone eras. Art lovers will delight in the array of street performers, local artisans, and open-air galleries that adorn the square, showcasing Bruges' vibrant cultural scene. Meanwhile, food connoisseurs will find themselves spoiled for choice with the plethora of cafes, restaurants, and food stalls offering a tantalizing array of Belgian delicacies and international cuisine.

What to Do

Markt offers a wealth of activities and attractions to suit every taste and interest. Visitors can start their exploration by admiring the towering Belfry of Bruges, which looms majestically over the square, offering panoramic views of the cityscape below. From there, they can wander among the market stalls, browsing for souvenirs, artisanal crafts, and locally-made goods to take home as cherished mementos of their visit. For those seeking a deeper dive into Bruges' history, guided tours of the square and its surrounding landmarks are available, providing valuable insights into the city's past and present.

Practical Tips for Visitors

Before embarking on a journey to Markt, it's advisable to check local event calendars and weather forecasts to ensure an enjoyable experience. Comfortable footwear and weather-appropriate clothing are essential, especially for those planning to spend extended periods exploring the square and its surroundings. Additionally, visitors should be mindful of their belongings and respectful of local customs and regulations, particularly during peak tourist seasons when crowds may be larger.

4.3 Basilica of the Holy Blood

Nestled within the cobbled streets of Bruges, Belgium, lies the Basilica of the Holy Blood—a sacred sanctuary steeped in history, spirituality, and architectural splendor. The Basilica of the Holy Blood stands as a cherished jewel in Bruges' crown, offering a sacred sanctuary for pilgrims, worshippers, and travelers alike.

Location and Accessibility

The Basilica of the Holy Blood is situated in the heart of Bruges' historic center, nestled within the Burg Square—a picturesque plaza adorned with majestic buildings and centuries-old charm. Accessible by foot from various points within the city, the basilica is easily reached by travelers exploring Bruges' enchanting streets on foot. For those arriving from farther afield, Bruges is well-connected by train, with the central station just a short distance from the city center. Additionally, bus services and guided tours offer convenient transportation options for visitors seeking to explore the region.

Entry Fee and Practical Information

One of the most enticing aspects of the Basilica of the Holy Blood is its accessibility to all, as there is no entry fee required to enter the basilica and pay homage to its sacred relics. Visitors are free to wander among the ornate chapels, admire the intricate craftsmanship of its architecture, and partake in moments of reflection and prayer without any financial barrier. However, donations are welcomed and appreciated to support the upkeep of this historic site and its religious artifacts.

Historical and Cultural Significance

The Basilica of the Holy Blood holds a revered place in Bruges' history and culture, serving as a testament to the city's deep-rooted Christian faith and spiritual traditions. Built in the 12th century, the basilica is renowned for housing a venerated relic—the purported cloth stained with the blood of Jesus Christ, brought to Bruges during the Crusades. This relic, known as the Holy Blood, has drawn pilgrims and worshippers from far and wide for centuries, making the basilica a cherished pilgrimage site and symbol of divine grace.

Why Visit?

Visiting the Basilica of the Holy Blood offers a profound and spiritually enriching experience for travelers of all backgrounds. Whether you're a devout believer seeking solace and inspiration or a curious traveler intrigued by the mysteries of faith, the basilica beckons with its sacred aura and timeless beauty. From the intricately carved altars to the shimmering stained glass windows, every corner of the basilica exudes an atmosphere of reverence and wonder, inviting visitors to pause and contemplate the mysteries of the divine.

What to Do

Upon entering the basilica, visitors can embark on a journey of spiritual discovery as they explore its hallowed halls and chapels, each adorned with exquisite religious artwork and artifacts. A highlight of any visit is the chance to behold the relic of the Holy Blood, housed within a jeweled reliquary and displayed for public veneration on designated occasions. Additionally, guided tours and audio guides are available for those seeking a deeper understanding of the basilica's history, architecture, and religious significance.

Practical Tips for Visitors

Before visiting the Basilica of the Holy Blood, it's advisable to check opening hours and any temporary closures due to religious ceremonies or maintenance. Modest attire is recommended out of respect for the sacred nature of the site, with shoulders and knees covered for both men and women. Photography may be restricted in certain areas, so visitors should be mindful of any signage or instructions from staff. Finally, visitors are encouraged to approach their visit with an open heart and mind, embracing the opportunity for quiet reflection and spiritual renewal.

4.4 Groeningemuseum

Tucked away in the picturesque city of Bruges, Belgium, lies a cultural treasure trove that beckons art enthusiasts and history buffs alike—the Groeningemuseum. Nestled in the historic center of Bruges, this museum stands as a testament to the city's rich artistic heritage and serves as a captivating window into the Flemish and Belgian art scene through the ages.

Location and Accessibility:

Situated at Dijver 12 in Bruges, Groeningemuseum enjoys a prime location near the bustling Markt square, making it easily accessible to visitors exploring the city's attractions. Whether you're strolling through cobblestone streets or cruising along the canals, the museum's central location ensures convenient access for tourists and locals alike.

Admission and Opening Hours:

Upon arrival, visitors can purchase tickets to gain entry to Groeningemuseum. While admission fees may vary based on age and residency status, the museum often offers discounted rates for students and seniors. It's advisable to check the official website for the latest ticket prices and any special exhibitions. The museum typically opens its doors from Tuesday to Sunday, with varying hours of operation. To make the most of your visit, it's recommended to plan your trip in advance and confirm the opening hours to avoid any disappointment.

Why Groeningemuseum is Worth Visiting:

Stepping into Groeningemuseum is akin to embarking on a captivating journey through the annals of art history. Renowned for its extensive collection of Flemish Primitive and Renaissance masterpieces, the museum offers a rare opportunity to admire works by celebrated artists such as Jan van Eyck, Hieronymus Bosch, and Hans Memling. Beyond its impressive roster of Flemish artworks, Groeningemuseum also boasts an eclectic selection of Belgian paintings spanning different genres and periods. From vibrant Baroque compositions to evocative Symbolist pieces, the museum's diverse exhibits showcase the evolution of Belgian artistry over the centuries.

Historical and Cultural Significance:

Founded in 1862, Groeningemuseum takes its name from the nearby Groeninge Abbey, which once occupied the site. Over the years, the museum has played a pivotal role in preserving and promoting Bruges' artistic heritage, serving as a cultural hub for locals and tourists alike. During the medieval period, Bruges flourished as a thriving mercantile center, attracting affluent patrons and skilled artisans from across Europe. This cultural melting pot laid the foundation for the city's vibrant artistic scene, with painters, sculptors, and craftsmen converging to create enduring masterpieces that adorn Groeningemuseum's halls today.

What to Do at Groeningemuseum:

Upon entering Groeningemuseum, visitors are greeted by a mesmerizing array of artworks that span multiple centuries and styles. Take your time to wander through the museum's well-curated galleries, each offering a unique perspective on the evolution of Flemish and Belgian art. Marvel at the intricate details of Jan van Eyck's iconic "Madonna with Canon van der Paele" or immerse yourself in the fantastical world of Hieronymus Bosch's "The Last Judgement." As you meander through the museum, don't miss the opportunity to discover lesser-known gems by emerging Belgian artists or temporary exhibitions that offer fresh insights into contemporary art trends. For those seeking a deeper understanding of the artworks on display, Groeningemuseum also offers guided tours and educational programs designed to enhance your museum experience. Engage with knowledgeable docents who can provide valuable insights into the historical context and artistic techniques behind each masterpiece.

Additional Information:

Before planning your visit to Groeningemuseum, it's essential to consider a few practicalities to ensure a seamless experience. Here are some additional tips to make the most of your time at the museum:

Photography: While photography is permitted in certain areas of the museum, be mindful of any restrictions and refrain from using flash photography to preserve the integrity of the artworks.

Accessibility: Groeningemuseum is committed to providing access to all visitors, with facilities in place to accommodate individuals with disabilities or special needs. If you require assistance during your visit, don't hesitate to reach out to museum staff for support.

Souvenirs and Amenities: Before bidding farewell to Groeningemuseum, don't forget to stop by the museum shop, where you'll find an array of art-inspired souvenirs, books, and gifts to commemorate your visit. Additionally, take advantage of the museum's onsite amenities, including restrooms and refreshment facilities, to recharge before continuing your exploration of Bruges.

4.5 Beguinage (Begijnhof)

Nestled amidst the cobblestone streets and medieval charm of Bruges, Belgium, lies a hidden oasis of tranquility—the Beguinage, also known as Begijnhof. This idyllic enclave offers visitors a serene escape from the bustling city center, inviting them to step back in time and immerse themselves in the peaceful ambiance of this historic site.

Location and Accessibility:

Situated on the outskirts of Bruges' city center, the Beguinage is conveniently located near the Minnewaterpark, making it easily accessible to visitors exploring the city's attractions. Whether you're strolling through the winding streets or cruising along the canals, the Beguinage's tranquil setting offers a serene respite from the urban hustle and bustle.

Admission and Opening Hours:

Unlike many tourist attractions, the Beguinage welcomes visitors free of charge, making it an accessible destination for travelers of all budgets. With no entry fee, visitors are free to wander through the peaceful grounds and soak in the tranquil atmosphere at their leisure. The Beguinage typically opens its gates to visitors during daylight hours, allowing ample time to explore the picturesque surroundings and learn about its fascinating history. It's advisable to check the opening hours in advance to plan your visit accordingly and avoid any disappointment.

Why Beguinage is Worth Visiting:

Stepping into the Beguinage is like entering a time capsule, transporting visitors back to the Middle Ages when devout women sought refuge in this serene sanctuary. This UNESCO World Heritage site offers a glimpse into the unique lifestyle of the Beguines, religious women who lived in semi-monastic communities dedicated to prayer, service, and simplicity. Beyond its historical significance, the Beguinage captivates visitors with its picturesque charm, boasting well-preserved rows of whitewashed houses, tranquil gardens, and a serene inner courtyard. Whether you're seeking solace amidst the lush greenery or capturing postcard-perfect photos, the Beguinage offers a peaceful retreat that's sure to leave a lasting impression.

Historical and Cultural Significance:

Founded in the 13th century, the Beguinage served as a refuge for women who wished to devote themselves to a life of piety and service without taking formal religious vows. These independent-minded women, known as Beguines, led a communal lifestyle centered around prayer, work, and charitable deeds, while also enjoying a degree of autonomy and independence uncommon for women of their time. Throughout the centuries, the Beguinage evolved into a thriving community, with its residents contributing to the cultural and social fabric of Bruges. Despite facing periods of upheaval and persecution, the Beguinage endured as a bastion of spirituality and solidarity, leaving behind a legacy that continues to inspire visitors to this day.

What to Do at Beguinage:

Upon entering the Beguinage, visitors are greeted by a sense of tranquility that permeates the air, inviting them to slow down and savor the moment. Take a leisurely stroll along the tree-lined pathways, admiring the charming architecture and serene gardens that characterize this historic enclave. As you explore the Beguinage, be sure to visit the Beguinage Church, a beautifully preserved Gothic structure that serves as the spiritual heart of the community. Step inside to marvel at the exquisite stained glass windows, ornate altars, and peaceful ambiance that fills this sacred space. For those seeking a deeper understanding of the Beguinage's history and significance, guided tours and informational exhibits are available to provide insights into the lives of the Beguines and their enduring legacy. Engage with knowledgeable guides who can offer fascinating anecdotes and historical context to enrich your visit.

Additional Information:

Before embarking on your journey to the Beguinage, here are a few practical tips to ensure a memorable experience:

Photography: While photography is permitted within the Beguinage, be mindful of your surroundings and respect the privacy of any residents or visitors. Capture the beauty of the landscape and architecture while being considerate of the peaceful atmosphere.

Quiet Reflection: As a place of spiritual significance, the Beguinage encourages visitors to maintain a respectful demeanor and observe moments of quiet reflection. Take the time to appreciate the serenity of your surroundings and soak in the timeless beauty of this historic site.

Accessibility: The Beguinage strives to provide access to all visitors, with wheelchair-friendly pathways and facilities available to accommodate individuals with disabilities or mobility challenges. If you require assistance during your visit, don't hesitate to reach out to the friendly staff for support.

4.6 Hidden Gems: Off-the-Beaten-Path Discoveries

While Bruges is renowned for its enchanting canals, medieval architecture, and bustling market squares, the city also harbors a wealth of hidden gems waiting to be discovered by intrepid travelers. Beyond the well-trodden tourist trails lie hidden treasures that offer a glimpse into Bruges' lesser-known attractions and off-the-beaten-path wonders.

Jerusalem Church (Jeruzalemkerk):

Tucked away in the southern outskirts of Bruges lies the Jerusalem Church, a hidden gem that boasts a rich history and breathtaking architectural splendor. Although slightly off the beaten path, this hidden treasure is well worth the visit for those seeking a unique cultural experience.

Admission and Opening Hours:

Entry to the Jerusalem Church typically requires a modest fee, which helps support the preservation efforts and maintenance of this historic site. Visitors can purchase tickets upon arrival or opt for guided tours, which offer deeper insights into the church's fascinating history and significance.

Why it is Worth Visiting:

The Jerusalem Church stands as a testament to Bruges' medieval heritage and serves as a captivating reminder of the city's religious and cultural diversity. Constructed in the 15th century by wealthy merchant families, the church was designed to replicate the holy sites of Jerusalem, featuring ornate Gothic architecture and intricate religious symbolism.

Historical and Cultural Significance:

Throughout the centuries, the Jerusalem Church has served as a place of pilgrimage and devotion for worshippers seeking spiritual solace and reflection.

Its awe-inspiring interior, adorned with stunning frescoes, marble sculptures, and a replica of Christ's tomb, offers a mesmerizing glimpse into the religious fervor and artistic craftsmanship of the era.

What to Do There:

Upon entering the Jerusalem Church, visitors are greeted by a sense of reverence and awe that permeates the air. Take a moment to admire the intricate details of the interior, including the exquisite stained glass windows, ornate altars, and sacred relics that adorn the sanctuary.

Additional Information:

Before planning your visit to the Jerusalem Church, it's advisable to check the opening hours and any special events that may be taking place. Additionally, be mindful of any dress codes or etiquette guidelines when visiting religious sites, and respect the sanctity of the space during your time there.

Sint-Janshospitaal (St. John's Hospital):

Nestled along the picturesque canals of Bruges lies the Sint-Janshospitaal, a hidden gem that offers a fascinating glimpse into the city's medieval healthcare system and charitable traditions. Despite its central location, this historic site often remains overlooked by tourists, making it a hidden treasure for discerning travelers to explore.

Admission and Opening Hours:

Entry to the Sint-Janshospitaal typically requires a modest fee, which helps support the preservation and maintenance of the hospital's historic buildings and collections. Visitors can purchase tickets on-site or opt for guided tours, which provide deeper insights into the hospital's storied past and enduring legacy.

Why it is Worth Visiting:

The Sint-Janshospitaal stands as a testament to Bruges' commitment to compassion and care, offering a poignant reminder of the city's medieval healthcare system and charitable endeavors. Founded in the 12th century by Countess of Flanders Margaret of Constantinople, the hospital provided shelter, sustenance, and medical treatment to the sick, injured, and destitute.

Historical and Cultural Significance:

Throughout its long history, the Sint-Janshospitaal played a vital role in the community, offering sanctuary to those in need and serving as a beacon of hope and healing amidst times of adversity. Its impressive architecture, including the iconic Hans Memling Museum housed within the hospital's chapel, showcases the rich artistic heritage and cultural significance of the site.

What to Do There:

Upon entering the Sint-Janshospitaal, visitors are transported back in time to an era of compassion and care, where the sick and infirm found solace and support in the embrace of the community. Wander through the hospital's historic halls and galleries, marveling at the stunning artworks and artifacts that chronicle its noble legacy.

Additional Information:

Before planning your visit to the Sint-Janshospitaal, it's advisable to check the opening hours and any special exhibitions or events that may be taking place. Additionally, be sure to explore the surrounding area, which is home to charming cafes, shops, and cultural attractions waiting to be discovered.

Bonifacius Bridge (Bonifaciusbrug):

Nestled along the tranquil canals of Bruges lies the Bonifacius Bridge, a hidden gem that offers breathtaking views of the city's iconic skyline and picturesque waterways. While easily accessible on foot or by bicycle, this hidden treasure often remains undiscovered by tourists, making it a secluded spot for peaceful contemplation and reflection.

Admission and Opening Hours:

Entry to the Bonifacius Bridge is free of charge, allowing visitors to enjoy its panoramic vistas and scenic beauty without any cost. Simply stroll along the canal pathways or cycle through the city's charming streets to reach this hidden gem, where you can soak in the enchanting ambiance and capture postcard-perfect photos of Bruges' timeless charm.

Why it is Worth Visiting:

The Bonifacius Bridge offers a unique vantage point from which to admire Bruges' architectural splendor and natural beauty, providing a tranquil retreat from the city's bustling crowds and tourist hotspots. Whether you're seeking a quiet moment of reflection or a romantic stroll along the canals, this hidden gem promises an unforgettable experience that's sure to leave a lasting impression.

Historical and Cultural Significance:

Constructed in the 20th century, the Bonifacius Bridge serves as a modern marvel of engineering and design, spanning the city's canals with grace and elegance. Its arched stone structure and charming lanterns evoke a sense of timeless beauty, harkening back to an era when Bruges was known as the "Venice of the North" for its network of waterways and bridges.

What to Do There:

Upon arriving at the Bonifacius Bridge, take a moment to pause and soak in the panoramic views of Bruges' enchanting skyline and historic landmarks. Watch as boats glide gracefully along the canals, framed by the backdrop of medieval buildings and quaint cobblestone streets.

Additional Information:

Before planning your visit to the Bonifacius Bridge, consider exploring the surrounding area, which is home to charming cafes, shops, and cultural attractions waiting to be discovered. Whether you're sampling Belgian delicacies or browsing for unique souvenirs, the streets of Bruges offer endless opportunities for exploration and discovery.

Astridpark:

Nestled in the heart of Bruges lies Astridpark, a verdant oasis that offers a welcome retreat from the city's bustling streets and historic landmarks. Despite its central location, this hidden gem remains relatively undiscovered by tourists, making it a tranquil haven for locals and visitors alike to enjoy.

Admission and Opening Hours:

Entry to Astridpark is free of charge, allowing visitors to explore its lush greenery and scenic beauty without any cost. Simply take a leisurely stroll through the park's winding pathways or find a quiet bench to relax and soak in the serene ambiance of this hidden treasure.

Why it is Worth Visiting:

Astridpark offers a peaceful respite from the hustle and bustle of Bruges' city center, inviting visitors to reconnect with nature and unwind amidst its idyllic surroundings. Whether you're enjoying a leisurely picnic with loved ones or taking a scenic walk through the park's verdant landscapes, this hidden gem promises a rejuvenating escape from the pressures of everyday life.

Historical and Cultural Significance:

Originally laid out in the 19th century, Astridpark has served as a beloved green space for generations of Bruges residents, providing a tranquil retreat for relaxation and recreation. Its well-manicured lawns, picturesque ponds, and charming bridges offer a timeless backdrop for leisurely activities and outdoor enjoyment.

What to Do There:

Upon entering Astridpark, take a moment to pause and appreciate the natural beauty that surrounds you, from the vibrant flora and fauna to the soothing sounds of rustling leaves and trickling water. Whether you're exploring the park's winding pathways, feeding the ducks in the pond, or simply basking in the sunshine, Astridpark offers endless opportunities for outdoor enjoyment and relaxation.

Additional Information:

Before planning your visit to Astridpark, consider bringing along a picnic lunch or snacks to enjoy amidst the park's scenic surroundings. Additionally, be sure to check the park's opening hours and any special events or activities that may be taking place during your visit.

De Halve Maan Brewery (Brouwerij De Halve Maan):

Nestled within the heart of Bruges lies De Halve Maan Brewery, a hidden gem that offers visitors a tantalizing glimpse into the city's rich brewing heritage and beer-making traditions. While centrally located, this historic brewery often remains undiscovered by tourists, making it a unique destination for beer enthusiasts and history buffs to explore.

Admission and Opening Hours:

Entry to De Halve Maan Brewery typically requires the purchase of a guided tour ticket, which includes access to the brewery's facilities and a tasting of its signature beers. Visitors can choose from a variety of tour options, ranging from standard guided tours to VIP experiences that offer exclusive access to special areas of the brewery.

Why it is Worth Visiting:

De Halve Maan Brewery offers a fascinating journey through the art and science of beer-making, allowing visitors to learn about the brewing process from start to finish. From the malting of grains to the fermentation of wort and the bottling of finished beers, this hidden gem offers a behind-the-scenes look at one of Belgium's most beloved beverages.

Historical and Cultural Significance:

Founded in 1856, De Halve Maan Brewery has played a pivotal role in shaping Bruges' beer culture and preserving its brewing traditions for future generations. The brewery's iconic tower, which overlooks the city's skyline, serves as a symbol of pride and craftsmanship, reflecting the dedication and passion of its founders and employees.

What to Do There:

Upon arriving at De Halve Maan Brewery, visitors are greeted by the inviting aroma of hops and barley, signaling the start of an unforgettable beer-tasting experience. Join a guided tour led by knowledgeable brewers who will walk you through the brewing process and share fascinating anecdotes about the brewery's history and heritage.

Additional Information:

Before planning your visit to De Halve Maan Brewery, it's advisable to book your tour in advance to secure your spot and avoid any disappointment. Additionally, be sure to check the brewery's opening hours and any special events or tastings that may be taking place during your visit.

CHAPTER 5

PRACTICAL INFORMATION AND TRAVEL RESOURCES

5.1 Maps and Navigation

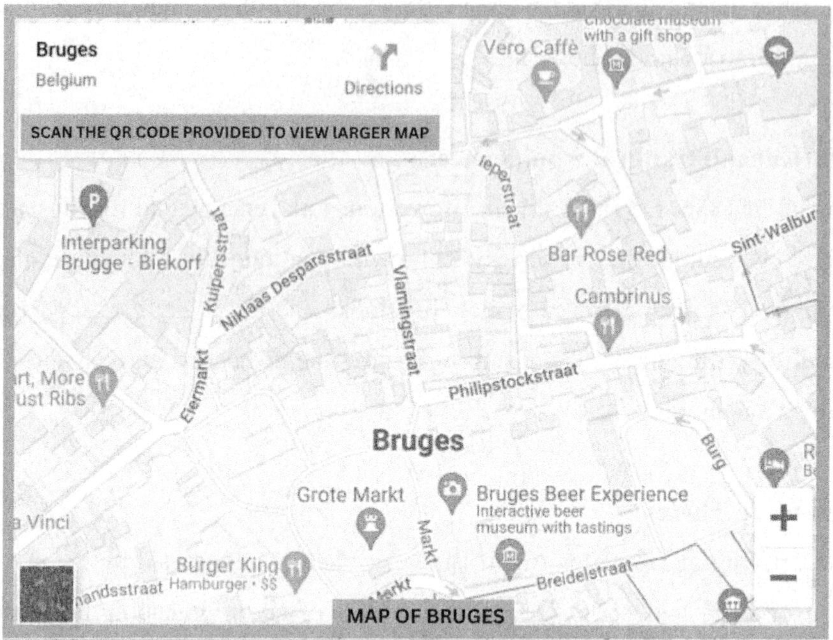

In the enchanting city of Bruges, navigating its labyrinthine streets and charming canals is an integral part of the travel experience. Whether you're exploring historic landmarks, quaint cobblestone alleys, or hidden treasures, having access to reliable maps and navigation tools is essential for making the most of your visit.

Bruges Tourist Map:

One of the most convenient and accessible ways to navigate Bruges is through the use of a tourist map. These maps, often available at hotels, visitor centers, and tourist information booths, provide an overview of the city's main attractions, landmarks, and points of interest. With clear markings and easy-to-follow directions, a Bruges tourist map serves as a handy companion for travelers looking to explore the city on foot or by bicycle. To access a physical tourist map in Bruges, simply inquire at your accommodation or visit one of the city's tourist information centers. These centers are typically located in central areas and offer a wealth of resources, including maps, brochures, and knowledgeable staff who can provide assistance and recommendations for your sightseeing adventures.

Digital Maps:

In addition to traditional paper maps, digital maps have become increasingly popular among modern travelers seeking convenience and flexibility in navigating unfamiliar destinations. With the rise of smartphones and mobile apps, accessing digital maps has never been easier, allowing travelers to explore Bruges with ease and confidence.

Accessing Digital Maps Offline:

For travelers who prefer offline navigation, several options are available for accessing digital maps in Bruges. Many mobile mapping apps, such as Google Maps (https://maps.google.com/) and Maps.me (https://maps.me/), offer the ability to download offline maps for use without an internet connection. Simply download the map of Bruges to your device before your trip, and you'll have access to detailed navigation information, including directions, points of interest, and offline search functionality.

Accessing Bruges' Maps Digitally:

For those seeking real-time navigation and up-to-date information, accessing Bruges' maps digitally is a convenient option. Numerous websites and travel apps provide comprehensive maps of the city, complete with interactive features, detailed landmarks, and customizable routes. Visitors can access these digital maps on their smartphones, tablets, or laptops, making it easy to plan their itinerary and navigate Bruges' streets with confidence. To provide readers with easy access to a comprehensive map of Bruges, consider including a link or QR code in your travel guidebook. This digital map can serve as a valuable resource for travelers, offering detailed insights into the city's layout, attractions, and transportation options. By clicking on the link or scanning the QR code, readers can instantly access the map from their mobile devices, allowing for seamless navigation and exploration of Bruges' hidden gems and must-see sights.

5.2 Essential Packing List

When preparing for a visit to Bruges, it's essential to pack clothing suitable for the city's climate and activities. Since Bruges experiences a maritime climate with cool summers and mild winters, it's advisable to pack clothings that can be easily added or removed depending on the weather. Bring comfortable walking shoes for exploring the cobblestone streets and consider packing a waterproof jacket or umbrella for rainy days. Additionally, Bruges' modest dress code may require covering shoulders and knees when visiting religious sites, so it's wise to pack lightweight, breathable clothing that provides coverage.

Accessories:

In addition to clothing, certain accessories can enhance your comfort and convenience during your visit to Bruges. Consider packing a day bag or backpack to carry essentials such as water bottles, snacks, sunscreen, and a camera for capturing memorable moments. Don't forget to bring a power adapter and portable charger to keep your electronic devices powered up while exploring the city. For those planning to cycle around Bruges, a bike lock and helmet are essential accessories for safety and security.

Travel Documents:

Before embarking on your journey to Bruges, ensure you have all necessary travel documents organized and easily accessible. This includes a valid passport or ID card for international visitors, as well as any required visas or travel permits. Don't forget to carry copies of important documents such as travel insurance, hotel reservations, and transportation tickets. It's also advisable to have a printed or digital map of Bruges and surrounding areas to aid navigation during your visit.

Personal Care Items:

To maintain your health and hygiene while traveling, pack a toiletry bag with essential personal care items. This may include items such as toothpaste, toothbrush, shampoo, conditioner, body wash, and skincare products. Don't forget to bring any prescription medications you may need, as well as over-the-counter remedies for common ailments such as headaches or allergies. Sunscreen and insect repellent are also important items to pack, especially during the summer months when spending time outdoors.

Miscellaneous Items:

In addition to the essentials mentioned above, there are several miscellaneous items that can enhance your comfort and convenience during your visit to

Bruges. Consider packing a reusable water bottle to stay hydrated while exploring the city, as well as a small travel umbrella or poncho for unexpected rain showers. A lightweight scarf or shawl can also be useful for adding warmth or modesty when visiting religious sites. Finally, don't forget to pack any specialty items or souvenirs you may wish to bring home from your trip to Bruges.

Packing for a visit to Bruges requires careful consideration of the city's climate, activities, and cultural norms. By packing essential clothing, accessories, travel documents, personal care items, and miscellaneous items, you can ensure a comfortable and enjoyable experience exploring this enchanting city. Remember to pack light, but be prepared for any weather or unexpected situations that may arise during your visit to Bruges.

5.3 Visa Requirements and Entry Procedures

As you embark on your journey to this enchanting destination situated in the heart of Belgium, it's essential to familiarize yourself with the visa requirements and entry procedures to ensure a seamless and enjoyable travel experience. Understanding the ins and outs of obtaining a visa, navigating immigration procedures, and adhering to customs regulations will help you navigate the process with confidence and ease.

Visa Requirements:

For travelers planning a visit to Bruges, it's essential to familiarize yourself with the visa requirements for entering Belgium, as Bruges is located within this European country. The specific visa requirements will vary depending on your nationality, the purpose of your visit, and the duration of your stay.

Schengen Visa:

Most visitors to Bruges will require a Schengen visa to enter Belgium, as Belgium is a member of the Schengen Area. The Schengen visa allows travelers to enter, stay, and travel freely within the Schengen Zone for up to 90 days within a 180-day period. To obtain a Schengen visa, travelers must submit an application to the Belgian embassy or consulate in their home country, along with supporting documents such as a valid passport, proof of accommodation, travel itinerary, and proof of sufficient funds to cover expenses during their stay.

Visa-exempt Countries:

Certain nationalities may be exempt from the Schengen visa requirement when visiting Belgium for short stays. Travelers from countries within the European Union (EU), European Economic Area (EEA), and Switzerland can enter Belgium without a visa for stays of up to 90 days within a 180-day period. Additionally, citizens of several other countries, including the United States, Canada, Australia, Japan, and many others, are visa-exempt for short stays in the Schengen Area.

Entry Procedures:

Upon arrival in Bruges, travelers must adhere to the entry procedures and requirements established by Belgian immigration authorities. This typically involves presenting a valid passport or ID card, along with any required visa or entry permit, to immigration officials at the port of entry. Visitors may also be asked to provide proof of sufficient funds, a return or onward ticket, and details of their accommodation during their stay in Bruges.

Customs Regulations:

In addition to immigration procedures, travelers should be aware of customs regulations when entering Belgium. Certain items may be subject to import restrictions or duties, including alcohol, tobacco, and goods exceeding certain value limits. It's advisable to familiarize yourself with Belgian customs regulations and declare any items of value or goods subject to restrictions upon arrival in Bruges.

Travel Insurance:

While not a visa requirement, travel insurance is highly recommended for visitors to Bruges. Travel insurance provides coverage for medical expenses, trip cancellations, lost luggage, and other unexpected events that may occur during your trip. Having adequate travel insurance can provide peace of mind and financial protection in the event of emergencies or unforeseen circumstances while traveling in Bruges.

Additional Information:

Before traveling to Bruges, it's advisable to check the latest visa requirements and entry procedures, as these may be subject to change. Contact the Belgian embassy or consulate in your home country for the most up-to-date information on visa applications, entry requirements, and travel advisories for Belgium.

5.4 Safety Tips and Emergency Contacts

Exploring the charming streets and historic landmarks of Bruges is a delightful experience filled with wonder and discovery. However, like any travel destination, it's important to prioritize safety and be prepared for emergencies while visiting this enchanting city in Belgium. By familiarizing yourself with safety tips and emergency contacts, you can ensure a safe and enjoyable journey through the cobblestone alleys and picturesque canals of Bruges.

Safety Tips:

Stay Aware of Your Surroundings:

While Bruges is generally considered a safe destination for travelers, it's essential to remain vigilant and aware of your surroundings, especially in crowded tourist areas. Keep an eye on your belongings and be cautious of pickpockets, particularly in busy markets, train stations, and popular attractions.

Use Reputable Transportation:

When traveling around Bruges, opt for reputable transportation options such as licensed taxis or public transit services. Be cautious when using unmarked taxis or accepting rides from strangers, and always verify the legitimacy of transportation providers to ensure your safety.

Secure Your Accommodation:

Choose reputable accommodations with secure locks and safety features to protect yourself and your belongings during your stay in Bruges. Keep valuables locked in a safe or secure location, and refrain from sharing personal information or room details with strangers.

Practice Responsible Drinking:

While enjoying Belgium's renowned beer culture, drink responsibly and avoid excessive alcohol consumption, which can impair judgment and increase vulnerability to accidents or incidents. Pace yourself, stay hydrated, and be mindful of your surroundings when socializing in bars or restaurants.

Follow Local Laws and Customs:

Respect local laws, customs, and cultural norms while visiting Bruges, including regulations regarding public behavior, alcohol consumption, and appropriate attire. Avoid engaging in illegal activities or disruptive behavior that could jeopardize your safety or impact your travel experience.

Emergency Contacts:

Emergency Services:

In case of emergencies, dial **112** for immediate assistance from police, fire, or medical services in Bruges and throughout Belgium. This universal emergency number is toll-free and accessible 24/7, providing prompt response to urgent situations.

Police:

For non-emergency police assistance or to report minor incidents, contact the local police station in Bruges. The Bruges Police Department can be reached at **+32 (0)50 44 88 88**, and officers are available to provide assistance and support to visitors as needed.

Medical Services:

In the event of a medical emergency or requiring medical assistance, seek help from healthcare facilities or hospitals in Bruges. The nearest hospital to the city center is AZ Sint-Jan Hospital, located at Ruddershove 10, 8000 Bruges. For non-emergency medical concerns, consult with local pharmacies or healthcare providers for guidance and assistance.

Embassy Contacts:

If you are a foreign national in need of consular assistance or support from your home country's embassy or consulate, contact the nearest diplomatic mission in Belgium. Embassy contact information can be found online or through official government websites, providing access to consular services and assistance for travelers in distress.

5.5 Currency, Banking, Budgeting and Money Matters

As you prepare for your journey to the enchanting city of Bruges, it's essential to familiarize yourself with currency, banking, budgeting, and money matters to ensure a smooth and hassle-free travel experience. From understanding the local currency to managing your finances and accessing banking services, having a comprehensive grasp of money matters in Bruges will empower you to make informed decisions and enjoy all that this captivating destination has to offer.

Currency:

The official currency of Belgium, including Bruges, is the Euro (EUR). Banknotes and coins denominated in euros are widely accepted throughout the city for transactions ranging from dining and shopping to transportation and attractions. It's advisable to obtain some euros before your trip or withdraw cash from ATMs upon arrival in Bruges to ensure you have local currency on hand for small purchases and emergencies.

Banking:

Bruges boasts a network of ATMs (Automated Teller Machines) conveniently located throughout the city, offering easy access to cash withdrawals and banking services. Major credit and debit cards, including Visa, Mastercard, and Maestro, are widely accepted at ATMs in Bruges, making it convenient for travelers to withdraw euros using their preferred payment method.

Banks and Exchange Offices:

In addition to ATMs, visitors to Bruges can utilize banks and exchange offices for currency exchange and financial services. Banks in Bruges typically operate on weekdays during standard business hours, with some branches offering extended hours or limited services on weekends. Exchange offices are also available in tourist areas and transportation hubs, providing currency exchange services for travelers in need of euros.

Budgeting:

While Bruges offers a range of accommodations, dining options, and attractions to suit various budgets, it's essential to budget wisely to make the most of your travel experience. The cost of living in Bruges can vary depending on factors such as accommodation type, dining preferences, and entertainment choices. By researching average prices for accommodations, meals, and activities in Bruges, you can create a realistic budget that aligns with your travel goals and financial resources.

Tips for Saving Money:

To stretch your budget further while visiting Bruges, consider adopting money-saving strategies such as dining at local eateries, shopping at markets or supermarkets for groceries and souvenirs, and taking advantage of free or low-cost attractions and activities. Additionally, booking accommodations in advance, purchasing multi-day attraction passes, and exploring on foot or by bicycle can help minimize expenses and maximize your enjoyment of Bruges without breaking the bank.

Money Matters:

Credit and debit cards are widely accepted for payments in Bruges, including hotels, restaurants, shops, and attractions. However, it's advisable to carry some cash for small purchases and transactions at establishments that may not accept cards or charge additional fees for card payments. Be sure to notify your bank of your travel plans to avoid any issues with card transactions while abroad.

Tipping:

Tipping is not obligatory in Belgium, as service charges are typically included in the bill at restaurants and cafes. However, if you receive exceptional service or wish to show appreciation, rounding up the bill or leaving a small tip is customary. Additionally, tipping taxi drivers and hotel staff for exceptional service is appreciated but not mandatory.

5.6 Language, Communication and Useful Phrases

As you prepare for your journey to the enchanting city of Bruges, understanding the local language, communication norms, and useful phrases will enhance your travel experience and facilitate interactions with locals. While Flemish (Dutch) is the official language of Belgium, including Bruges, English is widely spoken and understood, making it relatively easy for English-speaking visitors to communicate during their stay. However, embracing basic language skills and cultural etiquette can enrich your interactions and foster meaningful connections with the people of Bruges.

Language:

Flemish, a dialect of Dutch, is the predominant language spoken in Bruges and throughout Belgium. While learning Flemish may not be necessary for short-term visitors, familiarizing yourself with basic greetings, phrases, and common expressions can enhance your communication and cultural immersion during your stay. Locals appreciate efforts to speak their language, even if it's just a few words or phrases.

English:

English is widely spoken and understood in Bruges, particularly in tourist areas, hotels, restaurants, and attractions. Many locals, especially those working in the tourism industry, are proficient in English and can communicate effectively with English-speaking visitors. As a result, travelers can navigate Bruges with relative ease and confidence, relying on English as a common language for communication.

Cultural Etiquette:

While English is widely spoken in Bruges, it's essential to approach interactions with cultural sensitivity and respect for local customs and norms. When greeting locals, a friendly "hello" or "good morning" in Flemish (Dutch) such as "hallo" or "goedemorgen" can help establish rapport and demonstrate appreciation for the local language and culture.

Non-verbal Communication:

In addition to spoken language, non-verbal communication plays a significant role in interpersonal interactions in Bruges. Maintain eye contact, offer a warm smile, and use polite gestures such as nodding and handshakes to convey friendliness and respect. Being mindful of personal space and avoiding overly loud or boisterous behavior can also contribute to positive communication experiences.

Useful Phrases:

Basic Greetings:

Hello: ***Hallo***

Goodbye: ***Tot ziens***

Good morning: ***Goedemorgen***

Good afternoon: ***Goedemiddag***

Good evening: ***Goedenavond***

Common Phrases:

Please: ***Alstublieft***

Thank you: ***Dank u wel***

Excuse me: ***Excuseer me***

Yes: ***Ja***

No: ***Nee***

Directions and Assistance:

Where is...?: ***Waar is...?***

Can you help me?: ***Kunt u me helpen?***

I'm lost: ***Ik ben verdwaald***

How much does this cost?: ***Hoeveel kost dit?***

5.7 Useful Websites, Mobile Apps and Online Resources

Accessing reliable information and resources is essential for planning a memorable and enjoyable trip to the enchanting city of Bruges. Fortunately, Bruges boasts a wealth of useful websites, mobile apps, and online resources designed to assist visitors with everything from booking accommodations and navigating transportation to discovering hidden gems and exploring cultural attractions. By leveraging these digital tools, travelers can enhance their travel experience, streamline planning efforts, and make the most of their time in Bruges.

Planning Your Expedition:

Visit Bruges Official Website - The official tourism website of Bruges serves as a one-stop destination for comprehensive information on accommodations, attractions, dining options, events, and more. https://www.visitbruges.be/en

TripAdvisor - Utilize TripAdvisor to browse traveler reviews, recommendations, and insider tips on Bruges' top attractions, hotels, restaurants, and activities. The platform's robust community feedback ensures informed decision-making. https://www.tripadvisor.com/

Lonely Planet Bruges City Guide - Dive deep into Bruges' cultural tapestry with Lonely Planet's city guide. From historical insights to off-the-beaten-path discoveries, this resource offers invaluable insights for the discerning traveler. https://www.lonelyplanet.com/

Navigating the Terrain:

Google Maps - Trust Google Maps to navigate Bruges' labyrinthine streets with ease. Whether you're on foot, cycling, or using public transport, this app provides real-time directions, estimated travel times, and alternative routes. https://maps.google.com/

Bruges City Guide & Offline Map - Accessible offline, this app equips you with detailed maps, audio guides, and insider recommendations curated by locals. Say goodbye to connectivity woes as you explore Bruges' hidden gems. https://www.visitbruges.be/en

Moovit - Seamlessly integrate public transportation into your itinerary with Moovit. From bus schedules to tram routes, this app streamlines your commute, ensuring you maximize your time in Bruges. https://moovitapp.com/

Cultural Immersion and Exploration:

Bruges Museum Website - Immerse yourself in Bruges' rich heritage with the Bruges Museum App. Access multimedia guides, interactive maps, and curated tours of renowned museums, such as the Groeningemuseum and the Belfry of Bruges. https://www.museabrugge.be/en/

Rick Steves' Audio Europe - Enhance your sightseeing experience with Rick Steves' Audio Europe app. Listen to insightful audio tours of Bruges' iconic landmarks, narrated by the renowned travel expert himself. https://www.ricksteves.com/watch-read-listen/ ***(Available on Google Play Store and Apple Play Store)***

Clio Muse Tours - Delve into Bruges' history through engaging storytelling with Clio Muse Tours. From medieval marvels to architectural wonders, these digital tours offer a personalized exploration of the city's cultural heritage. https://cliomusetours.com/

Culinary Delights:

TheFork - Indulge your palate with TheFork, a comprehensive restaurant reservation platform offering diverse dining options in Bruges. Discover gastronomic gems, read reviews, and secure coveted tables with ease. https://www.thefork.com/

HappyCow - Embrace Bruges' vegetarian and vegan-friendly culinary scene with HappyCow. This app provides a directory of plant-based restaurants, cafes, and health food stores, ensuring a delectable dining experience for every palate. https://www.happycow.net/

BeerMenus - Navigate Bruges' vibrant beer culture with BeerMenus. From Trappist ales to artisanal brews, this app curates a comprehensive list of beer-centric establishments, allowing you to savor the city's liquid delights. https://www.beermenus.com/

Practical Essentials:

XE Currency Converter - Stay updated on currency exchange rates with XE Currency Converter. Whether you're splurging on Belgian chocolates or souvenir shopping, this app ensures you make informed financial decisions. https://www.xe.com/currencyconverter/

Weather Underground - Plan your outdoor excursions with precision using Weather Underground. This app provides hyper-local weather forecasts, ensuring you're prepared for Bruges' ever-changing climate. https://www.wunderground.com/

Google Translate - Bridge language barriers effortlessly with Google Translate. From deciphering menus to engaging with locals, this app offers instant translations in multiple languages, facilitating seamless communication during your Bruges escapade. https://translate.google.com/

5.8 Visitor Centers and Tourist Assistance

In Bruges, visitors can rely on a network of visitor centers and tourist assistance points to provide valuable support, information, and guidance throughout their stay. From the centrally located Bruges Tourist Information Center to convenient assistance points near transportation hubs and major attractions, travelers have access to comprehensive tourist services, including information, ticket sales, and assistance with accommodations and activities.

Bruges Tourist Office

Located in the heart of Bruges, the Bruges Tourist Office serves as the primary hub for visitor information and assistance. Situated at the historic Burg Square, this centrally located center offers a wealth of resources to ensure a memorable stay in the city.

Services Offered:

Multilingual staff providing personalized assistance and recommendations. Comprehensive brochures, maps, and guides covering attractions, accommodations, dining options, and events. Assistance with hotel bookings, restaurant reservations, and ticket purchases for attractions and activities. Access to free Wi-Fi and public restroom facilities. Souvenirs, postcards, and gifts available for purchase.

Bruges Information Desk at the Train Station

Conveniently located within the Bruges train station, the Information Desk caters to travelers arriving in the city by rail. Whether you need directions to your accommodation or insider tips on exploring Bruges, the friendly staff at this desk are ready to assist.

Services Offered:

Immediate assistance upon arrival, including guidance on transportation options, nearby attractions, and accommodations. Distribution of maps, brochures, and promotional materials to help visitors navigate the city. Information on train schedules, ticket purchases, and connections to other destinations in Belgium and beyond. Recommendations for dining, shopping, and sightseeing near the train station.

Mobile Tourist Information Points

For on-the-go assistance, keep an eye out for Bruges' Mobile Tourist Information Points stationed at key locations throughout the city center. These portable kiosks offer quick access to tourist information and can be found at popular landmarks and attractions, such as the Markt Square and the Belfry of Bruges.

Services Offered:

Instantaneous assistance from knowledgeable staff members fluent in multiple languages. Distribution of city maps, event calendars, and brochures highlighting nearby points of interest. Real-time updates on current events, festivals, and happenings in Bruges. Interactive displays and digital resources for self-guided exploration.

Digital Resources and Online Assistance

In addition to physical visitor centers and information points, Bruges offers a range of digital resources and online assistance to cater to the needs of modern travelers. The official Visit Bruges website (https://www.visitbruges.be/en) serves as a comprehensive online portal, providing up-to-date information, downloadable guides, and virtual tours to help visitors plan their Bruges experience from the comfort of their own homes. Website: Visit Bruges

Online Services:

Virtual assistance via live chat and email for inquiries and travel planning support. Access to digital maps, walking itineraries, and audio guides for self-guided exploration. Online booking platform for accommodations, guided tours, and cultural experiences. Social media channels for real-time updates, traveler testimonials, and community engagement.

CHAPTER 6

CULINARY DELIGHTS

6.1 Belgian Chocolates and Pralines

Belgian chocolates and pralines hold a prestigious status in the world of confectionery, renowned for their exquisite taste, rich flavors, and artisanal craftsmanship. Among the myriad of Belgian cities celebrated for their chocolate heritage, Bruges stands out as a quintessential destination for indulging in these delectable treats.

Exploration of Chocolate Shops:

Venturing through the enchanting lanes of Bruges, visitors are greeted by a symphony of aromas emanating from the numerous chocolate boutiques that line the streets. These establishments, ranging from quaint family-owned shops to upscale chocolatiers, showcase the diverse and irresistible creations of Belgian chocolatiers. Wandering into these emporiums, one is met with an opulent display of pralines, truffles, and chocolate bars, each meticulously crafted with skill and passion. The Market Square, or Markt, serves as a focal point for chocolate enthusiasts, boasting an array of renowned chocolate boutiques such as The Chocolate Line and Dumon Chocolatier. Here, visitors can immerse themselves in a sensory journey, sampling an assortment of chocolates infused with unique ingredients like exotic fruits, spices, and liqueurs. The ambiance of these establishments, characterized by warm lighting and elegant décor, elevates the chocolate tasting experience to a level of pure indulgence.

Praline Artistry and Innovation:

At the heart of Bruges' chocolate culture lies the art of praline-making, where chocolatiers showcase their creativity and ingenuity through intricate designs and flavor combinations. Pralines, with their delicate shells and sumptuous fillings, are a testament to the mastery of Belgian chocolatiers, who continuously push the boundaries of flavor and presentation. From classic combinations like hazelnut and caramel to avant-garde creations featuring sea salt and exotic spices, each praline tells a story of craftsmanship and innovation. Beyond the traditional pralines, Bruges' chocolatiers also offer a variety of chocolate sculptures and novelty items, perfect for gifts and souvenirs. Visitors can marvel at intricately crafted chocolate figurines depicting landmarks of Bruges or whimsical shapes inspired by nature and art. These edible works of art not only showcase the technical prowess of chocolatiers but also serve as a testament to the city's rich cultural heritage and artistic legacy.

Cultural Significance and Heritage:

The tradition of chocolate-making in Bruges dates back centuries, intertwining with the city's rich history and cultural identity. From the medieval era, when cocoa beans were introduced to Europe by Spanish explorers, to the present day, Bruges has remained at the forefront of chocolate craftsmanship, preserving age-old techniques while embracing innovation. Today, chocolate-making in Bruges is not merely a culinary pursuit but a cherished tradition passed down through generations, reflecting the city's commitment to excellence and quality.

6.2 Belgian Waffles and Pastries

Among the many culinary delights in Bruges, Belgian waffles and pastries hold a special place, enticing visitors with their irresistible aromas and decadent flavors. In the heart of this enchanting city, an array of establishments beckon travelers to indulge in these delectable treats, promising an unforgettable gastronomic experience.

Exploration of Waffle and Pastry Vendors:

Wandering through the cobblestone streets of Bruges, visitors are greeted by the tantalizing scent of freshly baked waffles wafting from numerous street vendors and quaint cafes. These vendors, often stationed in bustling squares like the Markt or along the scenic canals, offer an authentic taste of Belgian waffles, cooked to golden perfection and adorned with an array of toppings. Whether topped with strawberries and whipped cream or drizzled with decadent chocolate sauce, these waffles are a culinary delight not to be missed. In addition to street vendors, Bruges is home to a myriad of bakeries and pastry shops, each boasting its own unique selection of sweet treats. From traditional Belgian pastries like speculoos cookies and flaky buttery croissants to innovative creations incorporating local ingredients and flavors, these establishments cater to every craving and palate. Visitors can savor the delicate layers of a freshly baked mille-feuille or indulge in the creamy richness of a decadent éclair, all while soaking in the ambiance of Bruges' charming streets.

Cafes and Tea Rooms:

For those seeking a more leisurely dining experience, Bruges offers an abundance of cafes and tea rooms where waffles and pastries are served alongside a selection of fine beverages. Nestled within historic buildings or overlooking picturesque squares, these establishments provide the perfect setting to unwind and indulge in a sweet treat. Visitors can sip on fragrant teas or freshly brewed coffee while savoring a warm Belgian waffle dusted with powdered sugar, creating memories that linger long after the last crumb has been savored.

Cultural Significance and Heritage:

The tradition of waffle-making and pastry-baking in Belgium dates back centuries, with recipes passed down through generations and cherished as part of the country's culinary heritage. In Bruges, this tradition is celebrated with pride, as locals and visitors alike gather to enjoy these beloved delicacies in settings both modern and historic. From family-owned bakeries that have stood the test of time to innovative cafes pushing the boundaries of flavor and presentation, the waffles and pastries of Bruges reflect the city's rich cultural tapestry and commitment to culinary excellence.

6.3 Frites (Belgian Fries)

Belgian fries, or "frites," stand out as a quintessential street food experience in Bruges. These crispy golden fries, served with an array of delectable sauces, are a beloved staple of Belgian cuisine and a must-try for visitors exploring the gastronomic landscape of Bruges.

Exploration of Frite Stands and Shops:

As visitors meander through the enchanting streets of Bruges, they'll encounter an array of frite stands and shops, each offering their own take on this beloved snack. From bustling squares to hidden alleyways, the aroma of freshly fried potatoes fills the air, tempting passersby to indulge in a piping hot cone of frites. These establishments, often adorned with colorful signage and bustling with eager patrons, serve as gathering spots where locals and tourists alike come together to enjoy a shared culinary tradition. One iconic location for sampling Belgian fries in Bruges is the Markt, the city's central square. Here, visitors can find numerous frite stands offering freshly cooked fries served in a cone with a choice of sauces ranging from traditional mayonnaise to tangy Andalouse or spicy samurai sauce. The Markt's vibrant atmosphere, framed by historic architecture and bustling activity, provides the perfect backdrop for savoring this quintessential Belgian street food experience. Diving deeper into the city's culinary scene, visitors can also discover frite shops tucked away in quieter corners of Bruges. These establishments, often family-owned and operated, pride themselves on using high-quality potatoes and traditional frying methods to create fries with the perfect balance of crispiness and fluffy texture. Whether enjoyed on-the-go as a quick snack or paired with a hearty Belgian beer at a nearby cafe, Belgian fries offer a delicious taste of local culture and tradition.

Cultural Significance and Heritage:

The origins of Belgian fries can be traced back centuries, with some historians suggesting they were first introduced by 17th-century Belgian villagers who fried small fish to sustain themselves during harsh winters when rivers froze over. Over time, potatoes replaced fish as the primary ingredient, and Belgian fries grew in popularity, becoming a cherished part of the country's culinary heritage. In Bruges, the tradition of enjoying fries with friends and family is deeply ingrained in the local culture, with frite stands and shops serving as gathering places where people from all walks of life come together to share a meal and socialize. Whether enjoyed as a late-night snack after a night of revelry or as a leisurely afternoon treat, Belgian fries hold a special place in the hearts of Bruges' residents and visitors alike.

6.4 Belgian Beers and Breweries

Nestled within the medieval streets of Bruges lies a hidden gem for beer enthusiasts: the vibrant world of Belgian beers and breweries. Renowned for their rich flavors, complex aromas, and centuries-old brewing traditions, Belgian beers offer a tantalizing journey into the heart of Belgian culture. In Bruges, visitors have the opportunity to explore an array of breweries, taverns, and beer shops, each offering a unique glimpse into the diverse and dynamic world of Belgian brewing.

Exploration of Breweries and Tasting Rooms:

Bruges boasts a rich brewing heritage, with centuries-old breweries still crafting some of the world's finest beers. Visitors can embark on brewery tours to learn about the brewing process firsthand, from the selection of premium ingredients to the intricate techniques used to achieve distinct flavors and aromas. Guided tours often include tastings of a variety of beers, allowing visitors to sample traditional Belgian styles such as Trappist ales, Abbey beers, and sour ales, as well as innovative brews crafted by modern artisanal brewers. In addition to brewery tours, Bruges is home to numerous tasting rooms and beer cafes where visitors can immerse themselves in the diverse world of Belgian beers. These cozy establishments, adorned with rustic décor and shelves lined with an impressive selection of bottles and taps, offer the perfect setting to savor a pint or indulge in a beer tasting experience. Knowledgeable staff are on hand to guide visitors through the beer menu, providing insights into the different styles, brewing techniques, and flavor profiles that make Belgian beers so unique.

Beer Shops and Specialty Stores:

For those looking to take a piece of Belgian brewing heritage home with them, Bruges boasts a variety of beer shops and specialty stores where visitors can purchase a wide selection of Belgian beers to enjoy at their leisure. From quaint shops tucked away in historic alleyways to bustling market stalls in the city center, there are countless opportunities to discover and purchase a diverse array of brews, including limited-edition releases, seasonal specialties, and hard-to-find gems. Many beer shops in Bruges also offer expert advice and recommendations, helping visitors navigate the vast world of Belgian beers and find the perfect brew to suit their taste preferences. Whether seeking a crisp and refreshing blond ale, a robust and malty quadrupel, or a tart and fruity lambic, there's something for every palate waiting to be discovered in Bruges' beer shops and specialty stores.

Cultural Significance and Heritage:

Beer holds a special place in Belgian culture, with brewing traditions dating back centuries and beer consumption deeply ingrained in everyday life. In Bruges, this cultural significance is evident in the city's thriving beer scene, where historic breweries coexist alongside modern craft beer establishments, each contributing to the rich tapestry of Belgian brewing heritage.

6.5 Gastronomic Restaurants and Local Cuisine

Bruges, with its picturesque canals and medieval architecture, offers not only visual delights but also a culinary journey like no other. Amidst the cobblestone streets and historic landmarks, visitors can discover a treasure trove of gastronomic delights in the form of gastronomic restaurants serving up exquisite local cuisine. From traditional Flemish fare to innovative culinary creations, Bruges is a haven for food enthusiasts seeking to indulge in the flavors of Belgium.

De Karmeliet:

Tucked away in a charming corner of Bruges, De Karmeliet stands as a beacon of culinary excellence. Located in a historic building near the city center, this

Michelin-starred restaurant offers a refined dining experience that celebrates the rich flavors of Belgian cuisine with a modern twist. Chef Geert Van Hecke's innovative creations showcase the finest local ingredients, with dishes like North Sea turbot served with Belgian caviar and Flemish beef stew elevated to gourmet heights. Pair these culinary delights with an extensive wine list featuring both local and international selections, and indulge in an unforgettable dining experience. De Karmeliet is open for dinner from Tuesday to Saturday, with reservations recommended.

Den Gouden Harynck:

Nestled within the heart of Bruges' historic center, Den Gouden Harynck invites diners to embark on a culinary journey through the flavors of Flanders. This family-run restaurant, housed in a beautifully restored 17th-century townhouse, offers a warm and welcoming atmosphere perfect for savoring traditional Flemish dishes. From hearty stews and seafood specialties to decadent desserts like Belgian chocolate mousse, every dish at Den Gouden Harynck is crafted with care and attention to detail. Guests can complement their meal with a selection of Belgian beers or wines from the restaurant's well-curated list. Den Gouden Harynck is open for lunch and dinner from Wednesday to Sunday.

De Stove:

For a taste of authentic Belgian home cooking, look no further than De Stove. Located in a quaint residential neighborhood just a short walk from the city center, this cozy restaurant offers a warm and inviting atmosphere reminiscent of dining in a friend's kitchen. Chef-owner Peter De Clercq specializes in classic Flemish dishes made with locally sourced ingredients, such as beef stew with Belgian beer and mussels cooked in white wine and garlic. Guests can enjoy a relaxed dining experience with dishes served family-style, perfect for sharing and savoring the flavors of Belgium. De Stove is open for dinner from Wednesday to Sunday.

Park Restaurant:

Situated in the leafy surrounds of Bruges' Minnewater Park, Park Restaurant offers a tranquil setting for indulging in contemporary Belgian cuisine. Housed in a stylish glass-walled pavilion overlooking the park's scenic vistas, this upscale restaurant showcases the culinary talents of Chef Thierry Theys. Diners can expect inventive dishes that artfully blend traditional Belgian flavors with modern techniques, such as duck breast with cherry beer sauce and Belgian endive gratin. Complementing the menu is an extensive wine list featuring both local and international varietals, as well as a selection of craft beers. Park Restaurant is open for lunch and dinner from Tuesday to Saturday.

Bistro Refter:

Located in the heart of Bruges' historic center, Bistro Refter offers a cozy and intimate dining experience in a beautifully restored 14th-century building. The restaurant's rustic yet elegant interior sets the stage for enjoying classic Flemish dishes prepared with a contemporary twist. Chef Jürgen Aerts' menu features seasonal ingredients sourced from local producers, with dishes like Flemish carbonnade stew and grilled North Sea sole stealing the spotlight. Guests can pair their meal with a selection of Belgian beers or choose from the restaurant's curated wine list. Bistro Refter is open for lunch and dinner from Wednesday to Sunday.

De Vlaamsche Pot:

For a taste of traditional Flemish cuisine in a charming setting, De Vlaamsche Pot is a must-visit destination. Housed in a historic building with exposed wooden beams and cozy nooks, this family-run restaurant exudes warmth and hospitality. The menu showcases hearty Flemish classics such as beef stew with beer, stoofvlees, and rabbit in beer sauce, all served with generous portions of frites or mashed potatoes.

CHAPTER 7

CULTURE AND HERITAGE

7.1 Medieval Architecture in Bruges

Nestled in the heart of Belgium, the enchanting city of Bruges beckons visitors with its timeless charm and rich history. Renowned for its well-preserved medieval architecture, Bruges offers a captivating journey through the past, where every cobblestone street and towering spire tells a story of centuries gone by.

The Cityscape of Bruges

As you wander through the cobblestone streets of Bruges, you'll find yourself transported back in time to the medieval era. The cityscape is dominated by a tapestry of Gothic spires, picturesque canals, and meticulously preserved buildings that whisper tales of its illustrious past. From the majestic Belfry of Bruges, with its iconic octagonal tower, to the medieval guildhalls lining the Markt square, every corner of Bruges exudes an aura of antiquity and grandeur.

The Belfry of Bruges

Standing tall amidst the city's skyline, the Belfry of Bruges is a symbol of civic pride and architectural splendor. Ascend its narrow staircase, and you'll be rewarded with breathtaking panoramic views of the city below. Marvel at the intricate carvings adorning its facade and listen to the melodic chimes of its ancient bells, which have echoed through the streets of Bruges for centuries.

The Beguinage

Step into the serene oasis of the Beguinage, a tranquil retreat tucked away from the hustle and bustle of the city center. Originally founded in the 13th century as a sanctuary for religious women, the Beguinage is a testament to Bruges' medieval heritage. Wander through its peaceful courtyard, framed by rows of whitewashed houses and shaded by ancient trees, and you'll feel a sense of serenity wash over you.

The Church of Our Lady

Admire the graceful silhouette of the Church of Our Lady, whose towering spire pierces the sky and serves as a beacon for pilgrims and visitors alike. Built in the 13th century, this magnificent Gothic church is home to a treasure trove of artistic masterpieces, including the world-famous Madonna and Child sculpture by Michelangelo. Step inside its hallowed halls and marvel at the intricate stained glass windows and soaring vaulted ceilings that bear witness to Bruges' rich religious heritage.

The Canals of Bruges

Embark on a scenic boat tour along the tranquil canals of Bruges and discover the city's medieval marvels from a different perspective. Drift past charming bridges and waterfront mansions, as the gentle lapping of the water echoes the rhythm of time. Admire the quaint gabled houses that line the canal banks, their facades adorned with colorful shutters and blooming flower boxes, and feel the enchantment of Bruges envelop you.

7.2 Museums and Art Galleries

Bruges, often referred to as the "Venice of the North," not only captivates visitors with its picturesque canals and medieval architecture but also offers a rich cultural tapestry through its museums and art galleries.

Groeningemuseum

Located at Dijver 12, 8000 Bruges, the Groeningemuseum is a cultural gem nestled in the heart of the city. Opening its doors from Tuesday to Sunday, visitors can explore its extensive collection of Flemish and Belgian art spanning from the 15th to the 21st century. From iconic works by Jan van Eyck and Hieronymus Bosch to modern masterpieces by Rene Magritte, the Groeningemuseum offers a comprehensive overview of Bruges' artistic legacy. Admission fees vary depending on exhibitions, but generally range from €6 to €12.

Gruuthuse Museum

Situated at Dijver 17, 8000 Bruges, the Gruuthuse Museum invites visitors to step back in time and discover the opulent lifestyle of Bruges' medieval elite. Open daily except Mondays, this former palace showcases a dazzling array of decorative arts, including tapestries, silverware, and ceramics. Visitors can wander through its elegant halls and marvel at the exquisite craftsmanship on display. Admission to the Gruuthuse Museum is €12 for adults, with discounts available for students and seniors.

Memling Museum - Saint John's Hospital

Located at Mariastraat 38, 8000 Bruges, the Memling Museum housed within the historic Saint John's Hospital offers a fascinating journey into the life and works of the renowned Flemish painter Hans Memling. Open daily, visitors can admire a stunning collection of Memling's religious masterpieces, including his famous triptychs and altarpieces. The museum also provides insights into the hospital's medieval origins and its role in caring for the sick and needy. Admission to the Memling Museum is €12 for adults, with reduced rates for children and seniors.

Arentshuis

Situated at Dijver 16, 8000 Bruges, the Arentshuis is a hidden gem nestled along the picturesque canals of Bruges. Open daily except Mondays, this elegant townhouse showcases the works of Belgian artist Frank Brangwyn, as well as temporary exhibitions highlighting contemporary art and design. Visitors can explore its intimate galleries and tranquil garden, offering a peaceful respite from the bustling city streets. Admission to the Arentshuis is €8 for adults, with discounts available for students and seniors.

Beguinage Museum

Located at Begijnhof 24, 8000 Bruges, the Beguinage Museum provides a fascinating glimpse into the lives of Bruges' beguines, devout women who lived in community but without taking formal religious vows. Open daily, visitors can wander through the tranquil beguinage courtyard and explore the museum's exhibits showcasing artifacts, artworks, and archival materials related to beguinage life. Admission to the Beguinage Museum is €6 for adults, with reduced rates for children and seniors.

7.3 Lace Making and Crafts

Bruges, with its cobblestone streets and medieval charm, is not only renowned for its architectural marvels but also for its rich tradition of lace making and crafts. Steeped in history and craftsmanship, the city offers visitors a captivating journey into the intricate world of lace making and the vibrant tapestry of crafts that define its cultural identity.

Lace Making in Bruges:

Step into the world of lace making in Bruges, and you'll find yourself immersed in a tradition that dates back centuries. Known for its delicate beauty and meticulous craftsmanship, Bruges lace has been coveted by royalty and aristocracy alike. Visitors to the city can explore the Lace Center, located at Peperstraat 3, where they can witness skilled artisans at work, their nimble fingers weaving intricate patterns with precision and care. Guided tours and workshops offer visitors the opportunity to learn about the history of lace making in Bruges and even try their hand at creating their own masterpiece.

Exploring Craftsmanship in Bruges

Beyond lace making, Bruges is a haven for craftsmen and artisans practicing a variety of traditional crafts. Wander through the quaint streets of the city, and you'll discover workshops and boutiques showcasing a diverse array of handmade goods. From handcrafted chocolates and artisanal beers to intricately carved wooden figurines and exquisite pottery, Bruges celebrates craftsmanship in all its forms. Visitors can explore these workshops, chat with the artisans, and even purchase unique souvenirs to take home.

The Lace Museum:

For those eager to delve deeper into the history of lace making, a visit to the Lace Museum is a must. Housed within the historic Kantschool building at Balstraat 16, the museum offers a comprehensive overview of Bruges' lace making heritage. Visitors can admire an extensive collection of lace artifacts dating back centuries, including rare lace samples, tools, and equipment used by generations of lace makers. Interactive exhibits and multimedia displays bring the art of lace making to life, allowing visitors to appreciate the skill and artistry involved in this timeless craft.

Lace Festivals and Events

Throughout the year, Bruges hosts a variety of lace festivals and events that showcase the city's rich textile heritage. From the annual Bruges Lace Festival, where lace makers from around the world gather to exhibit their creations, to workshops and demonstrations held in conjunction with cultural celebrations, visitors have ample opportunities to immerse themselves in the world of lace making. These festivals not only celebrate the craft itself but also serve as a testament to its enduring significance in Bruges' cultural landscape.

7.4 Flemish Renaissance Art

The Flemish Renaissance, a golden age of artistic innovation and cultural flourishing, left an indelible mark on the art world of the 15th and 16th centuries. Nestled within the heart of Flanders, this vibrant period saw the emergence of a distinctive artistic style characterized by meticulous attention to detail, rich symbolism, and technical mastery. For visitors eager to immerse themselves in the splendor of Flemish Renaissance art, a journey through the historic cities of Bruges, Ghent, and Antwerp offers an unparalleled opportunity to witness these masterpieces firsthand.

The Ghent Altarpiece:

No exploration of Flemish Renaissance art would be complete without a pilgrimage to the St. Bavo's Cathedral in Ghent, home to the breathtaking Ghent Altarpiece. Created by the Van Eyck brothers, Jan and Hubert, this monumental polyptych is hailed as one of the greatest achievements of Western art. Admire the intricate panels depicting scenes from the Bible and marvel at the meticulous attention to detail, from the delicate folds of fabric to the luminous landscapes that seem to glow with divine light.

The Bruges Madonna:

In the tranquil halls of the Church of Our Lady in Bruges, visitors can behold another masterpiece of Flemish Renaissance art: Michelangelo's exquisite marble sculpture, the Bruges Madonna. Carved with unparalleled skill and sensitivity, this timeless work of art captures the Virgin Mary in a moment of serene contemplation, her gentle gaze and tender embrace conveying a sense of maternal love and grace that transcends the ages.

Rubenshuis:

In the bustling city of Antwerp, art enthusiasts can step into the world of Peter Paul Rubens, one of the most celebrated painters of the Flemish Renaissance. The Rubenshuis, once the private residence and studio of the artist, now serves as a museum dedicated to his life and work. Wander through the opulent chambers adorned with sumptuous tapestries and classical sculptures, and admire Rubens' masterful paintings, which pulsate with energy and vitality.

The Antwerp School:

While the Flemish Renaissance reached its zenith in the 16th century, its legacy continued to flourish into the Baroque period, as evidenced by the works of artists such as Anthony van Dyck and Peter Paul Rubens. The Antwerp School, renowned for its dynamic compositions and emotive realism, produced a wealth of masterpieces that continue to captivate audiences to this day. Visitors to Antwerp can explore the city's numerous museums and galleries, where these iconic works are proudly displayed.

7.5 Festivals and Events in Bruges

Bruges, with its medieval charm and cultural richness, plays host to a myriad of festivals and events throughout the year, each offering a unique opportunity for visitors to immerse themselves in the vibrant tapestry of the city's heritage.

From colorful parades to culinary celebrations, Bruges' calendar is brimming with experiences that captivate the senses and ignite the imagination.

The Procession of the Holy Blood:

One of Bruges' most iconic events, the Procession of the Holy Blood, takes place on Ascension Day, usually in May. This centuries-old tradition commemorates the arrival of the relic of the Holy Blood to Bruges in the 12th century. The procession features elaborate floats, costumed participants, and reenactments of biblical scenes, creating a breathtaking spectacle that transports spectators back in time. With its rich historical significance and vibrant pageantry, the Procession of the Holy Blood is a must-see event that offers a captivating glimpse into Bruges' religious heritage.

Bruges Beer Festival:

For beer enthusiasts, the Bruges Beer Festival held in February is a can't-miss event that celebrates Belgium's rich brewing tradition. Set against the backdrop of the historic Belfry of Bruges, this festival brings together over 400 Belgian beers from renowned breweries across the country. Visitors can sample a diverse array of brews, from traditional Trappist ales to innovative craft beers, while enjoying live music and culinary delights. With its festive atmosphere and unparalleled selection of beers, the Bruges Beer Festival offers a true taste of Belgian hospitality and craftsmanship.

Cactusfestival:

Music lovers flock to Bruges in July for the Cactusfestival, a three-day music extravaganza held in the picturesque Minnewaterpark. Featuring an eclectic lineup of international and local artists spanning various genres, from indie rock to electronic dance music, the Cactusfestival promises a melodic journey amidst lush greenery and tranquil lakes. With its laid-back ambiance and stunning natural setting, this festival offers the perfect opportunity to soak up the summer sun while enjoying world-class performances under the open sky.

Bruges Christmas Market:

As the holiday season approaches, Bruges transforms into a winter wonderland with its enchanting Christmas Market, held from late November to early January. The historic Markt square and surrounding streets are adorned with twinkling lights, festive decorations, and charming wooden chalets selling traditional crafts, seasonal treats, and warming mulled wine. Visitors can ice skate on the picturesque rink, listen to carolers singing holiday classics, and marvel at the dazzling displays of lights and decorations that adorn the city's medieval landmarks. With its magical ambiance and festive cheer, the Bruges Christmas Market is a joyous celebration of the holiday season that enchants visitors of all ages.

Bruges Triennial:

Every three years, Bruges plays host to the Bruges Triennial, an international exhibition of contemporary art and architecture held from May to September. Against the backdrop of the city's historic landmarks and picturesque canals, visitors can discover thought-provoking installations and site-specific artworks created by leading artists and designers from around the world. From interactive sculptures to immersive multimedia experiences, the Bruges Triennial offers a unique opportunity to explore the intersection of art, culture, and urban space. With guided tours, artist talks, and special events, the triennial invites visitors to engage with art in unexpected ways and discover Bruges from a fresh perspective.

CHAPTER 8

OUTDOOR ACTIVITIES AND ADVENTURES

8.1 Biking and Cycling Routes

Bruges, with its winding canals and cobblestone streets, is not only a delight to explore on foot but also offers a plethora of cycling routes that allow visitors to discover the city and its surrounding countryside at their own pace. From leisurely rides along picturesque canals to more challenging routes through verdant landscapes, there's something for every cyclist to enjoy in Bruges.

Bruges City Center:

Begin your cycling journey in the heart of Bruges, where narrow streets and medieval architecture create a charming backdrop for exploration. Rent a bike from one of the many rental shops located near the Market Square and set off to discover iconic landmarks such as the Belfry of Bruges, the Church of Our

Lady, and the tranquil Beguinage. Pedal along the picturesque canals lined with gabled houses and graceful bridges, pausing to admire the scenery and snap photos of this UNESCO World Heritage Site.

Bruges to Damme:

For a leisurely cycling excursion, follow the scenic route from Bruges to the charming village of Damme, located just a few kilometers northeast of the city. The flat, well-maintained path follows the tranquil canal, offering panoramic views of the surrounding countryside and glimpses of quaint windmills along the way. Upon reaching Damme, park your bike and explore the village's cobbled streets, historic buildings, and cozy cafes before retracing your route back to Bruges.

Bruges to the Coast:

For more adventurous cyclists, the route from Bruges to the Belgian coast offers a thrilling journey through coastal landscapes and seaside towns. Follow the well-marked cycling paths that wind through scenic polders and nature reserves, passing through charming villages such as Zeebrugge and Blankenberge along the way. Arrive at the bustling seaside resort of Knokke-Heist, where you can relax on the sandy beaches, indulge in fresh seafood, and soak up the vibrant atmosphere before heading back to Bruges.

Bruges to Lissewege:

Venture off the beaten path and discover the rural beauty of Flanders on a cycling excursion from Bruges to the idyllic village of Lissewege. The route takes you through picturesque farmland and pastoral landscapes, with opportunities to spot grazing cows, rustic farmhouses, and colorful flower fields. Upon reaching Lissewege, explore its well-preserved medieval architecture, visit the historic church of Our Lady, and savor local specialties at a charming village pub before pedaling back to Bruges.

Bruges to the Damme Forest:

Escape the hustle and bustle of the city and immerse yourself in nature on a cycling adventure to the Damme Forest, located just a short distance from Bruges. Follow the peaceful cycling paths that wind through dense woodlands, tranquil ponds, and meandering streams, where you can spot wildlife such as deer, rabbits, and a variety of bird species. Take a break to relax amidst the serene surroundings, enjoy a picnic lunch, or explore the forest trails on foot before returning to Bruges refreshed and rejuvenated.

8.2 Walking Tours and Nature Trails

Bruges offers visitors an array of walking tours and nature trails to explore the city and its surrounding countryside. From leisurely strolls through historic city streets to invigorating hikes in scenic nature reserves, there's something for everyone to enjoy on foot in Bruges.

Historic City Center Walking Tour:

Embark on a guided walking tour of Bruges' historic city center and immerse yourself in the rich tapestry of the city's past. Begin at the iconic Markt square, where the towering Belfry of Bruges offers panoramic views of the city skyline. Wander through narrow cobblestone streets lined with medieval buildings, pausing to admire landmarks such as the Church of Our Lady and the tranquil Beguinage. Learn about Bruges' fascinating history, from its role as a prosperous trading hub to its cultural renaissance during the Flemish Golden Age, as you explore the city's charming alleys and hidden courtyards.

Canal Walk:

Take a leisurely stroll along Bruges' picturesque canals and discover the city's unique waterways from a different perspective. Start at the Dijver canal near the Groeningemuseum and follow the meandering paths that wind through the heart of the city. Admire the graceful bridges and gabled houses that line the water's edge, and watch as swans glide gracefully across the tranquil waters. Along the way, you'll pass historic landmarks such as the Gruuthuse Museum and the picturesque Rozenhoedkaai, where you can capture postcard-perfect views of Bruges' iconic skyline reflected in the water.

Minnewater Park:

Escape the hustle and bustle of the city and retreat to the serene surroundings of Minnewater Park, located just a short walk from the city center. Follow the winding paths that meander through lush greenery, past tranquil ponds and graceful swans. Marvel at the romantic charm of the Minnewater Lake, where according to legend, a lovelorn maiden named Minna met her tragic fate. Admire the graceful arches of the Lover's Bridge and take a moment to relax amidst the tranquil beauty of this idyllic oasis.

Bruges Woodlands:

For those seeking a more adventurous outing, the Bruges Woodlands offer a variety of hiking trails and nature walks to explore. Head to the outskirts of the city and embark on a scenic hike through dense forests, rolling hills, and open meadows. Follow well-marked trails that lead to hidden gems such as the Tillegem Castle and the Tudor-era Tudor Walk. Keep an eye out for wildlife such as deer, rabbits, and a variety of bird species as you immerse yourself in the natural beauty of the Bruges countryside.

Zwin Nature Park:

Venture beyond the city limits and discover the coastal wonders of Zwin Nature Park, located just a short drive from Bruges. Follow walking trails that wind through salt marshes, dunes, and tidal flats, offering spectacular views of the North Sea coast. Learn about the park's unique ecosystem and its importance as a habitat for migratory birds and other wildlife. Explore interactive exhibits, observation platforms, and bird hides that allow visitors to observe nature up close and gain a deeper appreciation for the biodiversity of the Zwin region.

8.3 Boating and Kayaking on the Canals

Immerse yourself in the enchanting beauty of Bruges by taking to the waterways that crisscross this medieval city. Boating and kayaking on the canals offer visitors a unique and memorable way to experience Bruges' picturesque scenery, historic landmarks, and tranquil ambiance.

Boat Tours:

Embark on a guided boat tour and let the gentle rhythm of the water transport you through the heart of Bruges' historic city center. Board one of the charming canal boats, known as "reien," at designated docking points such as Rozenhoedkaai or Huidenvettersplein. Sit back and relax as your knowledgeable guide navigates the maze of canals, regaling you with fascinating tales of Bruges' rich history and architectural treasures. Marvel at the elegant facades of centuries-old buildings reflected in the shimmering waters, and admire iconic landmarks such as the Belfry of Bruges, the Church of Our Lady, and the medieval guildhalls that line the canals.

Kayaking Adventures:

For a more immersive and active experience, embark on a kayaking adventure and explore Bruges' canals at your own pace. Rent a kayak from one of the outfitters located near the city center and set off to discover hidden corners and quiet waterways that are inaccessible by larger boats. Paddle beneath graceful bridges and through charming canal locks, soaking up the serene atmosphere and admiring the city's architectural gems from a unique vantage point. Keep an eye out for swans, ducks, and other wildlife that call the canals home, and feel a sense of tranquility as you glide through the waterways surrounded by the timeless beauty of Bruges.

Sunset Cruises:

As the sun dips below the horizon, experience the magic of Bruges at twilight on a sunset cruise along the canals. Settle into a cozy boat with your loved one or a group of friends and savor the romantic ambiance as the city lights twinkle against the dusky sky. Watch as the buildings along the canal banks are bathed in the warm glow of the setting sun, creating a truly enchanting atmosphere. Toast to unforgettable moments and cherished memories as you cruise through the heart of Bruges, where every turn reveals a new vista of beauty and tranquility.

Practical Information:

Before embarking on a boating or kayaking adventure in Bruges, there are a few practical considerations to keep in mind. Boat tours typically operate from spring to autumn, with varying schedules and durations depending on the tour provider and weather conditions. It's advisable to book your tour in advance, especially during peak tourist seasons, to secure your preferred time slot. For kayaking, rental shops provide all necessary equipment, including life jackets and paddles, and offer instructions for beginners. Additionally, be mindful of other canal traffic and follow safety guidelines while navigating the waterways.

8.4 Picnicking in Bruges' Parks

Bruges, with its charming parks and green spaces, offers visitors the perfect setting for a delightful picnic experience amidst the city's historic beauty and natural tranquility. Whether you're seeking a romantic rendezvous, a family outing, or a peaceful escape from the hustle and bustle of city life, Bruges' parks provide idyllic spots for picnicking and relaxation.

Minnewater Park:

Nestled in the heart of Bruges, Minnewater Park beckons visitors with its serene ambiance and picturesque landscapes. Spread out a blanket on the lush grassy lawns beside the tranquil Minnewater Lake, where graceful swans glide gracefully across the shimmering waters. Take a leisurely stroll along the winding paths that meander through verdant greenery, past blooming flowers and towering trees. Find a quiet spot beneath the shade of a weeping willow or beside a charming bridge, and savor a picnic feast amidst the tranquil beauty of this idyllic oasis.

Koningin Astridpark:

Tucked away from the bustling city center, Koningin Astridpark offers a peaceful retreat for picnickers seeking solitude and relaxation. Explore the park's beautifully landscaped gardens, featuring colorful flower beds, scenic ponds, and charming sculptures. Find a secluded spot beneath the shade of a tree or beside a tranquil fountain, and enjoy a leisurely picnic surrounded by the sights and sounds of nature. With plenty of benches and picnic tables scattered throughout the park, Koningin Astridpark provides the perfect setting for a leisurely outdoor meal with family and friends.

Sint-Andriespark:

For a scenic picnic experience with a touch of romance, head to Sint-Andriespark, located along the banks of the picturesque Coupure canal. Spread out a blanket on the grassy riverbank and admire the tranquil waters as boats glide by and sunlight dances on the surface. Take a leisurely stroll along the tree-lined pathways that wind through the park, offering panoramic views of the canal and surrounding greenery. Pack a picnic basket with your favorite snacks and refreshments, and enjoy a relaxing meal in the serene ambiance of Sint-Andriespark.

Veltembos:

Escape the urban hustle and immerse yourself in nature at Veltembos, a sprawling forested area located on the outskirts of Bruges. Discover peaceful picnic spots amidst dense woodlands, babbling brooks, and scenic meadows, where you can enjoy a rustic outdoor meal surrounded by the sights and sounds of the forest. Explore hiking trails that wind through the woods, offering glimpses of wildlife and stunning views of the countryside. With designated picnic areas equipped with tables and benches, Veltembos provides the perfect setting for a nature-inspired picnic adventure.

What Visitors Need to Know

Before embarking on a picnic adventure in Bruges' parks, there are a few practical considerations to keep in mind. Pack a picnic basket with your favorite snacks, sandwiches, and beverages, as well as a blanket or picnic mat for seating. Remember to bring along essentials such as sunscreen, insect repellent, and garbage bags to ensure a comfortable and responsible picnic experience. Additionally, be mindful of park regulations regarding alcohol consumption, waste disposal, and designated picnic areas.

8.5 Day Trips to the Belgian Coast

Escape the medieval charm of Bruges and embark on a day trip to the Belgian coast, where sandy beaches, bustling promenades, and charming seaside towns await. Just a short distance from Bruges, the Belgian coast offers visitors the perfect opportunity to relax, unwind, and soak up the sun amidst stunning coastal scenery.

Ostend:

Located approximately 25 kilometers northwest of Bruges, Ostend is the largest and most popular seaside resort on the Belgian coast. Easily accessible by train or car, Ostend boasts a wide sandy beach, lively promenade, and vibrant city center. Spend the day lounging on the beach, building sandcastles, or taking a refreshing dip in the North Sea. Stroll along the bustling promenade lined with cafes, restaurants, and shops, and savor fresh seafood specialties such as shrimp croquettes and mussel pots. Don't miss the chance to explore Ostend's cultural attractions, including the Mercator Ship Museum, the Fort Napoleon, and the James Ensor House.

Blankenberge:

Situated just 15 kilometers west of Bruges, Blankenberge is a charming seaside resort known for its family-friendly atmosphere and lively entertainment options. Hop on a train or take a short drive to Blankenberge, where you'll find a wide sandy beach, bustling boardwalk, and a variety of attractions for all ages. Treat the kids to a day of fun at the Sea Life Blankenberge aquarium, where they can marvel at marine creatures from around the world. Take a leisurely stroll along the bustling Zeedijk promenade, where colorful beach huts, amusement arcades, and souvenir shops line the seafront. Afterward, relax on the beach with a picnic or enjoy a meal at one of the seaside restaurants overlooking the North Sea.

Knokke-Heist:

For a more upscale seaside experience, head to Knokke-Heist, located approximately 20 kilometers northeast of Bruges. Accessible by train or car, Knokke-Heist is known for its upscale boutiques, chic beach clubs, and exclusive villas. Spend the day lounging on the pristine beach, where luxurious sun loungers and cabanas await. Explore the fashionable boutiques and designer shops along the bustling Lippenslaan and Dumortierlaan shopping streets, or indulge in a spa treatment at one of the area's upscale wellness centers. Afterward, dine al fresco at one of Knokke-Heist's gourmet restaurants, where fresh seafood and fine wines are served with impeccable style and hospitality.

De Haan:

Located approximately 20 kilometers southwest of Bruges, De Haan is a quaint seaside town known for its Belle Epoque architecture, pristine beaches, and tranquil ambiance. Accessible by train or car, De Haan offers a more laid-back alternative to the bustling resorts of Ostend and Blankenberge. Take a leisurely stroll along the picturesque promenade, lined with elegant villas and charming cafes, and soak up the nostalgic charm of this seaside gem. Spend the day sunbathing on the sandy beach, exploring the dunes, or swimming in the refreshing waters of the North Sea. Don't miss the opportunity to visit the historic tram station, where you can take a ride on a vintage tram and experience the nostalgia of bygone eras.

Zeebrugge:

Situated just 15 kilometers northwest of Bruges, Zeebrugge is a bustling port town known for its maritime heritage, sandy beaches, and lively harbor. Accessible by train or car, Zeebrugge offers visitors the chance to explore the bustling port area, where cargo ships, ferries, and cruise liners dock. Relax on the sandy beach, where you can soak up the sun, go for a swim, or try your hand at water sports such as windsurfing and kiteboarding. Explore the maritime attractions of Zeebrugge, including the Seafront Maritime Theme Park, the Zeebrugge Beach Memorial, and the iconic Pier and Lighthouse. After a day of exploration, dine at one of the waterfront restaurants, where you can enjoy fresh seafood and panoramic views of the harbor.

What Visitors Need to Know

When planning a day trip to the Belgian coast from Bruges, there are a few practical considerations to keep in mind. Check train schedules and ticket prices in advance, as well as parking options if traveling by car. Pack sunscreen, beach towels, and plenty of water for a day of sun and fun at the beach.

CHAPTER 9

SHOPPING IN BRUGES

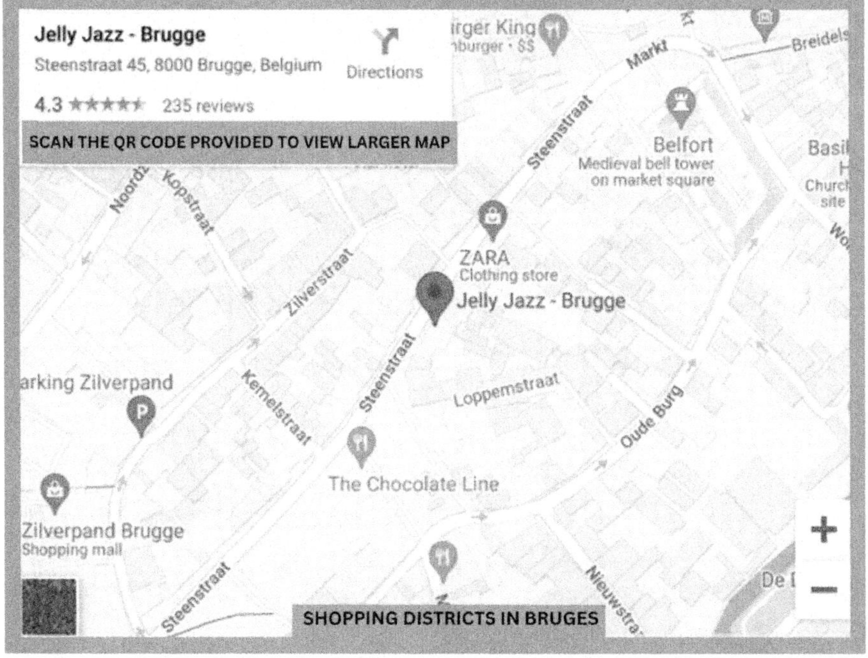

SCAN THE QR CODE PROVIDED TO VIEW LARGER MAP

Scan the QR Code with a device to view a comprehensive and larger map of Shopping Districts in Bruges

SHOPPING DISTRICTS IN BRUGES

9.1 Belgian Chocolate Shops

Nestled within the cobblestone streets and medieval architecture of Bruges lie hidden gems of indulgence - Belgian chocolate shops that beckon both locals and visitors alike with their exquisite offerings. These chocolatiers not only showcase the rich tradition of Belgian chocolate-making but also offer a delightful sensory journey for those with a penchant for all things sweet.

The Chocolate Line:

Located in the heart of Bruges, The Chocolate Line stands as a testament to the innovative spirit within Belgian chocolate craftsmanship. Founded by Dominique Persoone, a renowned chocolatier known for his daring flavor combinations, The Chocolate Line offers a unique fusion of traditional Belgian techniques with avant-garde flair. Visitors are welcomed into a whimsical world of chocolate artistry, where they can witness firsthand the meticulous process of chocolate creation. With an array of unconventional flavors such as wasabi, bacon, and even tobacco-infused chocolate, The Chocolate Line promises a sensory adventure unlike any other.

Praline:

For those seeking the timeless elegance of classic Belgian pralines, Praline is the quintessential destination. Tucked away in a charming corner of Bruges, this boutique chocolatier epitomizes the essence of Belgian chocolate tradition. Here, visitors can indulge in a selection of impeccably crafted pralines, each delicately handcrafted with precision and passion. From velvety ganaches to crunchy nougats, Praline offers a symphony of flavors that pay homage to centuries-old recipes passed down through generations. With its warm ambiance and personalized service, Praline provides a truly enchanting chocolate experience for all who enter its doors.

The Old Chocolate House:

Stepping into The Old Chocolate House is akin to embarking on a journey through the annals of chocolate history. Housed within a historic building dating back to the 17th century, this iconic chocolate shop exudes charm and nostalgia at every turn. Here, visitors can immerse themselves in the time-honored tradition of Belgian chocolate-making, with a wide selection of artisanal chocolates and truffles to tantalize the taste buds. From velvety milk chocolate to intense dark cocoa, The Old Chocolate House offers something for every chocolate aficionado. Additionally, guests can partake in chocolate workshops and tastings, gaining insight into the craftsmanship behind each delectable creation.

Dumon Chocolatier:

Nestled along the bustling streets of Bruges, Dumon Chocolatier stands as a beacon of excellence in the world of Belgian chocolate. Founded by the Dumon family over a century ago, this esteemed chocolatier has garnered acclaim for its unwavering commitment to quality and tradition. Here, visitors can sample an array of artisanal chocolates, each meticulously crafted using only the finest ingredients sourced from around the globe. From silky-smooth pralines to decadent chocolate bars, Dumon Chocolatier offers a taste of luxury that has stood the test of time. With its warm hospitality and timeless elegance, Dumon Chocolatier invites guests to savor the simple pleasures of life through the art of chocolate-making.

Neuhaus:

Founded in 1857, Neuhaus is a true pioneer in the world of Belgian chocolate, renowned for its innovative creations and impeccable craftsmanship. Located in the heart of Bruges, Neuhaus invites visitors to discover a world of indulgence where tradition meets innovation. With its signature pralines and truffles, each meticulously crafted to perfection, Neuhaus offers a sensory experience like no other. Additionally, guests can explore the brand's rich heritage through guided tours and tastings, gaining insight into the artistry behind each delectable treat. Whether indulging in a classic praline or savoring a contemporary creation, a visit to Neuhaus promises to awaken the senses and ignite the imagination.

Navigating Your Chocolate Journey in Bruges

As you embark on your chocolate-filled adventure in Bruges, it's essential to plan your itinerary wisely to ensure you don't miss out on any of these delightful experiences. Begin your journey by exploring the historic streets of Bruges, taking in the sights and sounds of this enchanting city. Then, make your way to each of these esteemed chocolatiers, allowing ample time to savor the exquisite flavors and immerse yourself in the rich heritage of Belgian chocolate-making. Don't forget to indulge in a chocolate workshop or tasting session, where you can gain insight into the artistry behind each delectable creation. Lastly, be sure to pick up some souvenirs to take home, allowing you to savor the memories of your chocolate-filled adventure in Bruges for years to come.

9.2 Lace and Linen Stores

Nestled amidst the picturesque cobblestone streets and medieval architecture of Bruges are a plethora of charming boutiques offering exquisite lace and linen creations. These stores, steeped in tradition and craftsmanship, invite visitors to embark on a journey of elegance and sophistication, where every thread tells a story of timeless beauty.

‘t Apostelientje:

Located in the heart of Bruges, ‘t Apostelientje stands as a beacon of tradition in the world of lace and linen. This quaint boutique, tucked away in a historic building, specializes in handmade lace and embroidered linens that reflect the rich heritage of Belgian craftsmanship. Visitors are welcomed into a world of intricate designs and delicate fabrics, where each piece tells a tale of artistry and dedication. Whether seeking a timeless tablecloth or a delicate lace handkerchief, ‘t Apostelientje offers a curated selection of treasures that capture the essence of Bruges’ textile tradition.

Kantcentrum:

For those eager to delve deeper into the art of lace-making, a visit to Kantcentrum is a must. Situated within a former lace school dating back to the 19th century, Kantcentrum serves as a living testament to Bruges’ rich lace-making heritage. Here, visitors can marvel at an extensive collection of exquisite lace pieces, ranging from intricate doilies to ornate shawls, all meticulously crafted by local artisans. Additionally, guests have the opportunity to witness live lace-making demonstrations, providing insight into the intricate techniques passed down through generations. With its educational exhibits and interactive workshops, Kantcentrum offers a captivating glimpse into the intricate world of lace craftsmanship.

The Bruges Diamond:

Stepping into The Bruges Diamond is akin to entering a realm of opulence and luxury. Located in a historic mansion in the heart of Bruges, this prestigious linen boutique showcases an array of sumptuous linens fit for royalty. From plush bath towels to exquisitely embroidered bedding, The Bruges Diamond offers a selection of linens crafted from the finest materials sourced from around the world. Visitors can indulge in personalized shopping experiences, with expert staff on hand to assist in selecting the perfect pieces to complement their home decor. With its regal ambiance and impeccable attention to detail, The Bruges Diamond promises a shopping experience worthy of its name.

Lace Corner:

Situated in a charming corner of Bruges, Lace Corner seamlessly blends traditional craftsmanship with contemporary design. This boutique, housed within a historic building, showcases a curated collection of lace and linen creations that marry heritage techniques with modern sensibilities. Visitors can peruse an array of beautifully crafted lace garments, from intricate dresses to delicate accessories, each reflecting a unique fusion of past and present. Additionally, Lace Corner offers bespoke tailoring services, allowing guests to create custom pieces tailored to their individual tastes. With its commitment to innovation and quality, Lace Corner offers a fresh perspective on Bruges' timeless textile tradition.

De Witte Pelikaan:

For those seeking a comprehensive selection of linens and textiles, De Witte Pelikaan is a veritable haven. Located in a historic building dating back to the 18th century, this expansive store offers an extensive range of linens, ranging from luxurious bedding to elegant tablecloths. Visitors can explore multiple floors filled with an array of fabrics, each carefully curated to cater to every discerning taste. With its attentive staff and commitment to quality, De Witte Pelikaan ensures a shopping experience that is both indulgent and memorable. Whether stocking up on household essentials or searching for the perfect gift, a visit to De Witte Pelikaan is sure to delight even the most discerning shopper.

Embarking on a Textile Adventure in Bruges

As you navigate the enchanting streets of Bruges in search of lace and linen treasures, be sure to allow ample time to explore each boutique and immerse yourself in the rich textile heritage of the city. From traditional lace-making demonstrations to personalized shopping experiences, Bruges offers a wealth of opportunities to discover the elegance and craftsmanship of Belgian textiles. Whether seeking a timeless keepsake or a contemporary masterpiece, these boutiques promise an unforgettable shopping experience that celebrates the artistry and tradition of lace and linen-making in Bruges.

9.3 Antique Markets and Artisanal Crafts

Nestled within the cobblestone streets and historic squares of Bruges are a plethora of antique markets and artisanal craft shops, each offering a treasure trove of unique finds and timeless creations. These hidden gems invite visitors to embark on a journey of discovery, where every corner reveals a new delight waiting to be unearthed.

De Snuffel:

Tucked away in the heart of Bruges, De Snuffel stands as a mecca for vintage enthusiasts and collectors alike. This bustling market boasts an eclectic array of treasures, ranging from antique furniture and decor to vintage clothing and accessories. Visitors can lose themselves amidst the maze of stalls, each brimming with one-of-a-kind finds waiting to be discovered. With its lively atmosphere and ever-changing inventory, De Snuffel promises an unforgettable shopping experience for those with a penchant for the past. To get there, visitors can simply stroll through the city center, following the signs to the Markt square where De Snuffel is located nearby.

Brocante Markt:

For a taste of Bruges' rich history and heritage, a visit to the Brocante Markt is a must. Held in various locations throughout the city, this beloved flea market offers an enchanting glimpse into the past, with vendors selling an array of antique goods and curiosities. From vintage books and ephemera to retro homeware and collectibles, the Brocante Markt is a treasure trove waiting to be explored. Visitors can soak in the sights and sounds of this vibrant market as they meander through the stalls, uncovering hidden gems and lost treasures along the way. The market's locations vary, so visitors are advised to check local listings or ask at their accommodation for upcoming dates and venues.

Galerie Kreo:

Situated in a historic building in the heart of Bruges, Galerie Kreo showcases the work of local artisans and craftsmen, offering a curated selection of handmade goods and artistic creations. From handcrafted jewelry and pottery to intricate woodwork and textiles, Galerie Kreo celebrates the beauty of traditional craftsmanship in a contemporary setting. Visitors can browse the gallery at their leisure, admiring the skill and creativity of Bruges' talented artisans. Additionally, the gallery often hosts special exhibitions and events, providing an opportunity to meet the makers and learn more about their craft. Galerie Kreo is conveniently located near the Gruuthuse Museum, making it easily accessible to visitors exploring the city center.

De Witte Raaf:

For those seeking a blend of artistry and antiquity, De Witte Raaf offers a curated selection of vintage and artisanal goods that embody the essence of Bruges' cultural heritage. Located in a historic building near the Burg square, this charming shop exudes old-world charm, with its collection of antique furniture, artwork, and decorative objects. Visitors can peruse the carefully curated displays, each showcasing a unique blend of craftsmanship and history. Whether searching for a statement piece for their home or a unique souvenir to commemorate their trip, guests are sure to find something special at De Witte Raaf.

Howest Kortrijkstraat:

Nestled along the bustling Kortrijkstraat, Howest is a vibrant hub of creativity and innovation, showcasing the work of students from the local art and design school. Here, visitors can explore a diverse range of handmade goods, from contemporary artwork and sculptures to bespoke jewelry and accessories. With its dynamic atmosphere and ever-changing exhibitions, Howest offers a unique shopping experience that celebrates the talent and creativity of Bruges' up-and-coming artists. To reach Howest, visitors can take a leisurely stroll through the city center or hop on a local bus to Kortrijkstraat, where the school is located.

Embarking on a Journey of Discovery in Bruges

As visitors meander through the charming streets and squares of Bruges, they are invited to immerse themselves in the city's rich cultural tapestry, where antiquity and artistry converge to create a truly enchanting shopping experience. From bustling flea markets to quaint artisanal shops, Bruges offers a wealth of opportunities to unearth hidden treasures and discover the beauty of handmade craftsmanship. Whether seeking a vintage souvenir or a contemporary masterpiece, visitors are sure to find inspiration around every corner in this magical city.

9.4 Souvenir Shops and Gift Stores

In the heart of Bruges, amidst its cobblestone streets and medieval architecture, lie charming souvenir shops and gift stores beckoning visitors to take home a piece of the city's enchanting spirit. Each of these establishments offers a unique selection of mementos and treasures, ensuring that every visitor finds the perfect keepsake to commemorate their time in Bruges.

The Chocolate Line:

Nestled in the bustling city center, The Chocolate Line stands as a haven for chocolate aficionados seeking the perfect souvenir. While primarily known for its delectable chocolates, The Chocolate Line also offers an array of beautifully packaged chocolate bars, pralines, and truffles, making it an ideal destination for those looking to bring home a taste of Bruges. Visitors can indulge in a sensory journey through the shop's offerings, sampling unique flavors and browsing through elegant gift sets. Conveniently located near the Markt square, The Chocolate Line is easily accessible to visitors exploring the city center.

Gruuthuse Souvenir Shop:

Located within the historic Gruuthuse Museum, the Gruuthuse Souvenir Shop offers an array of souvenirs and gifts inspired by Bruges' rich cultural heritage. From intricately crafted replicas of medieval artifacts to locally made crafts and trinkets, the shop provides visitors with an opportunity to take home a piece of Bruges' history. Additionally, guests can explore the museum's exhibits before or after their shopping excursion, gaining insight into the city's past and enhancing their souvenir-shopping experience. Situated near the Burg square, the Gruuthuse Souvenir Shop is easily accessible to visitors exploring the city center.

The Lace Corner:

For those seeking a souvenir that exudes elegance and sophistication, The Lace Corner offers a curated selection of lace and linen products that showcase Bruges' textile tradition. From delicate lace handkerchiefs to intricately embroidered tablecloths, the shop boasts an array of timeless treasures that capture the essence of Bruges' craftsmanship. Visitors can browse through the shop's offerings, admiring the intricate designs and impeccable craftsmanship of each piece. Conveniently located in the city center, The Lace Corner is a must-visit destination for those looking to bring home a piece of Bruges' textile heritage.

De Witte Pelikaan:

Situated in a historic building near the Markt square, De Witte Pelikaan offers an extensive selection of linens and textiles that make for elegant souvenirs or gifts. From plush bath towels and cozy throws to intricately woven tapestries, the shop showcases a variety of products designed to add a touch of luxury to any home. Visitors can explore the shop's multiple floors, perusing the selection of fabrics and accessories before selecting the perfect souvenir to take home. With its convenient location and wide range of products, De Witte Pelikaan provides visitors with an opportunity to bring a piece of Bruges' textile heritage into their own homes.

The Old Chocolate House:

Stepping into The Old Chocolate House is like stepping into a chocolate lover's paradise, where every corner is adorned with delectable treats waiting to be savored. While primarily known for its artisanal chocolates, The Old Chocolate House also offers an array of souvenir-worthy items, including chocolate bars, truffles, and gift sets. Visitors can explore the shop's whimsical interior, sampling chocolates and browsing through the selection of gifts before selecting the perfect memento to take home. Located near the bustling Markt square, The Old Chocolate House is a convenient stop for visitors exploring the city center.

9.5 Fashion Boutiques and Designer Stores

As visitors explore the vibrant streets of Bruges, they'll find an array of fashion boutiques and designer stores waiting to be discovered. Whether seeking contemporary chic or high-end luxury, Bruges offers a diverse range of options for fashion shopping, ensuring that every visitor finds the perfect pieces to elevate their wardrobe. With its convenient locations and curated selections, fashion shopping in Bruges is not just a transaction but an experience to be savored and remembered for years to come.

LolaLiza: Situated in the bustling city center, LolaLiza stands as a beacon of contemporary chic, offering a versatile range of apparel and accessories for every occasion. From casual basics to statement pieces, the boutique caters to a diverse clientele seeking stylish yet accessible fashion. Visitors can peruse racks filled with on-trend clothing, including dresses, tops, and outerwear, as well as a selection of accessories to complete their look. Conveniently located near the Markt square, LolaLiza is easily accessible to visitors exploring the city center, making it a must-visit destination for fashion enthusiasts.

Veritas:

For those seeking the perfect finishing touch to their ensemble, Veritas offers a curated selection of accessories that add flair and personality to any outfit. Located in the heart of Bruges, this boutique specializes in a wide range of accessories, including jewelry, scarves, handbags, and hair accessories. Visitors can explore the shop's offerings, browsing through shelves adorned with sparkling baubles and colorful scarves before selecting the perfect accessories to complement their look. With its convenient location and affordable prices, Veritas is a popular destination for fashion-conscious visitors looking to accessorize with style.

Bluepoint:

Situated in a historic building near the Burg square, Bluepoint caters to discerning clientele seeking luxury labels and high-end fashion. The boutique boasts an impressive selection of designer clothing and accessories from renowned fashion houses, including Armani, Gucci, and Prada. Visitors can explore racks adorned with haute couture creations, from tailored suits and elegant dresses to statement handbags and footwear. With its sophisticated ambiance and impeccable service, Bluepoint offers a shopping experience worthy of its prestigious offerings. To reach Bluepoint, visitors can take a leisurely stroll through the city center or opt for a taxi for added convenience.

Hilde Devolder:

For a taste of Belgian elegance and sophistication, Hilde Devolder offers a curated selection of timeless designs crafted from luxurious fabrics and impeccable tailoring. Located in a charming corner of Bruges, this boutique showcases the work of Belgian designers known for their commitment to quality and craftsmanship. Visitors can peruse racks filled with elegant dresses, chic separates, and statement outerwear, each exuding understated glamour and refinement. Additionally, Hilde Devolder offers personalized styling services, allowing guests to create bespoke looks tailored to their individual tastes. With its intimate ambiance and exquisite offerings, Hilde Devolder provides a shopping experience that celebrates the artistry of Belgian fashion.

CHAPTER 10

DAY TRIPS AND EXCURSIONS

10.1 Ghent: City of Altarpieces

Nestled within the picturesque landscape of Belgium lies Ghent, a city steeped in history, culture, and architectural marvels. For visitors staying in Bruges, a day trip to Ghent offers a tantalizing glimpse into another facet of Belgium's rich heritage, particularly its renowned altarpieces. From exploring medieval castles to wandering along scenic canals, a day trip to Ghent promises a memorable adventure filled with art, culture, and culinary delights.

Journeying from Bruges to Ghent:

Embarking on a day trip to Ghent from Bruges is a relatively straightforward endeavor, with multiple transportation options available. Visitors can opt to travel by train, with frequent departures from Bruges' main railway station to Ghent's central station, Ghent-Sint-Pieters. The journey takes approximately

30-40 minutes, offering scenic views of the Belgian countryside along the way. Alternatively, travelers can choose to drive to Ghent, with the journey typically taking around 45 minutes via the E40 highway. Once in Ghent, navigating the city is convenient, with an extensive network of trams, buses, and taxis readily available to transport visitors to their desired destinations.

Ghent's Magnificent Altarpieces:

Upon arriving in Ghent, visitors are greeted by a city adorned with architectural splendors and artistic treasures, with the city's altarpieces serving as a focal point of its cultural heritage.

The Mystic Lamb:

Arguably one of the most iconic altarpieces in the world, the Mystic Lamb, also known as the Ghent Altarpiece, finds its home within the awe-inspiring confines of St. Bavo's Cathedral. Created by the Van Eyck brothers, Hubert and Jan van Eyck, in the 15th century, this monumental polyptych mesmerizes visitors with its intricate detail and sublime beauty. The altarpiece consists of 12 panels depicting various scenes from the Bible, including the Adoration of the Mystic Lamb at its center. Located in the heart of Ghent's historic center, St. Bavo's Cathedral is easily accessible by foot or public transportation, making it a must-visit destination for art aficionados and history enthusiasts alike.

The Adoration of the Magi:

Another masterpiece hailing from Bruges and now residing in Ghent is "The Adoration of the Magi" by the renowned Flemish painter, Hugo van der Goes. This exquisite altarpiece, originally commissioned for the Carmelite church in Bruges, is now housed in the Museum of Fine Arts in Ghent. The altarpiece captivates viewers with its rich colors, intricate detailing, and emotional depth, showcasing van der Goes' mastery of the Flemish Renaissance style. Visitors to Ghent can immerse themselves in the beauty of this iconic artwork by exploring the Museum of Fine Arts, conveniently located near the city center and easily accessible by public transportation.

St. John Altarpiece:

The St. John Altarpiece, attributed to the workshop of the celebrated Bruges painter Hans Memling, is yet another treasure that found its way from Bruges to Ghent. Originally created for the hospital chapel of St. John in Bruges, this polyptych masterpiece now resides in the Museum of Fine Arts in Ghent. Comprising multiple panels depicting scenes from the life of St. John the Baptist, the altarpiece enchants visitors with its delicate brushwork, vibrant colors, and intricate symbolism. Located in the heart of Ghent, the Museum of Fine Arts offers visitors the opportunity to admire this remarkable artwork up close, providing insight into Bruges' artistic legacy and its influence on Ghent's cultural landscape.

10.2 Brussels: Capital of Belgium

Embarking on a day trip from Bruges to Brussels offers visitors a captivating journey into the heart of Belgium's vibrant capital city. Bursting with history, culture, and culinary delights, Brussels promises an unforgettable experience for travelers eager to immerse themselves in its rich tapestry of art, architecture, and gastronomy.

Getting to Brussels from Bruges:

Traveling from Bruges to Brussels is convenient and efficient, with multiple transportation options available. The most popular choice is by train, with frequent services departing from Bruges Railway Station to Brussels Central Station. The journey typically takes around 1 hour and 10 minutes, offering travelers a comfortable and scenic ride through the picturesque Belgian countryside. Tickets can be purchased at the station or online through the

Belgian Rail website or mobile app. Alternatively, visitors can opt to travel by car, with the journey between Bruges and Brussels taking approximately 1 hour and 15 minutes via the E40 highway. Parking in Brussels can be challenging, so it's advisable to use public parking facilities or opt for park-and-ride options on the outskirts of the city and explore Brussels on foot or by public transportation.

Exploring Brussels' Iconic Landmarks:

Upon arrival in Brussels, visitors are greeted by an array of iconic landmarks and attractions waiting to be discovered. One of the city's most famous landmarks is the Grand Place, a UNESCO World Heritage site renowned for its stunning architecture, including the magnificent Town Hall and opulent guild houses. Visitors can stroll through the square, admiring the intricate facades and soaking in the vibrant atmosphere of this historic hub. Nearby, the Manneken Pis statue, a beloved symbol of Brussels, captures the hearts of visitors with its whimsical charm. Located just a short walk from the Grand Place, this iconic bronze sculpture of a little boy urinating is a must-see attraction that embodies the city's playful spirit.

Cultural Delights and Artistic Marvels:

For art enthusiasts, a visit to the Royal Museums of Fine Arts of Belgium offers a journey through centuries of artistic mastery. Home to a vast collection of European paintings, including works by Flemish masters such as Rubens and Bruegel, the museum provides a captivating glimpse into Belgium's rich artistic heritage. Food lovers will delight in Brussels' culinary scene, with its abundance of street markets, chocolate shops, and gastronomic delights waiting to be savored. From indulging in decadent Belgian chocolates to sampling traditional Belgian waffles and frites, Brussels offers a feast for the senses that is sure to satisfy even the most discerning palate.

Embracing Brussels' Multicultural Spirit:

As the capital of Belgium and the seat of the European Union, Brussels boasts a diverse and multicultural population that adds to its dynamic energy and cosmopolitan charm. Visitors can explore neighborhoods such as the Marolles and Saint-Gilles, where trendy boutiques, eclectic cafes, and vibrant street art reflect the city's diverse cultural tapestry.

10.3 Antwerp: Diamond Capital

Embarking on a day trip from Bruges to Antwerp offers visitors a fascinating journey into the heart of Belgium's vibrant diamond capital. Renowned for its rich history, thriving cultural scene, and world-class architecture, Antwerp beckons travelers with its eclectic mix of old-world charm and modern sophistication.

Getting to Antwerp from Bruges:

Traveling from Bruges to Antwerp is convenient and straightforward, with several transportation options available. The most common way to reach Antwerp from Bruges is by train, with frequent services departing from Bruges Railway Station to Antwerp Central Station. The journey typically takes around 1 hour and 15 minutes, offering travelers a comfortable and scenic ride through the picturesque Belgian countryside. Tickets can be purchased at the station or online through the Belgian Rail website or mobile app. Alternatively, visitors can choose to travel by car, with the journey between Bruges and Antwerp taking approximately 1 hour and 30 minutes via the E34 highway. Parking in Antwerp can be challenging, so it's advisable to use public parking facilities or opt for park-and-ride options on the outskirts of the city and explore Antwerp on foot or by public transportation.

Exploring Antwerp's Iconic Landmarks:

Upon arrival in Antwerp, visitors are greeted by a plethora of iconic landmarks and attractions waiting to be discovered. One of the city's most famous landmarks is the majestic Cathedral of Our Lady, a UNESCO World Heritage site renowned for its stunning Gothic architecture and awe-inspiring interior. Visitors can marvel at the cathedral's towering spire and intricate stained glass windows, providing a glimpse into Antwerp's rich religious heritage. Nearby, the historic Grote Markt (Great Market Square) captivates visitors with its picturesque charm and vibrant atmosphere. Lined with beautiful Renaissance and Baroque-style guild houses, the square is a hub of activity, boasting outdoor cafes, lively street performers, and a bustling market selling fresh produce and local delicacies.

Diamond District:

No visit to Antwerp would be complete without exploring its famed Diamond District, known as the "Diamond Capital of the World." Situated near Antwerp Central Station, this bustling district is home to a vast array of diamond dealers, jewelers, and diamond workshops, making it a paradise for gem enthusiasts and luxury shoppers alike. Visitors can stroll along the streets lined with glittering storefronts, admiring exquisite diamond jewelry and sparkling gemstones on display.

Cultural Delights and Artistic Marvels:

For art enthusiasts, a visit to Antwerp's Museum aan de Stroom (MAS) offers a journey through the city's rich cultural heritage. Located along the waterfront in the trendy Eilandje district, the museum showcases a diverse collection of art, artifacts, and exhibits that highlight Antwerp's maritime history, global connections, and contemporary culture. From ancient artifacts to modern masterpieces, the MAS provides a fascinating glimpse into Antwerp's past, present, and future.

Embracing Antwerp's Multicultural Flavor:

As Belgium's second-largest city and one of Europe's most diverse metropolises, Antwerp boasts a vibrant multicultural population that adds to its dynamic energy and cosmopolitan charm. Visitors can explore neighborhoods such as the trendy Zurenborg district, known for its eclectic mix of architectural styles, hip cafes, and multicultural eateries. Here, visitors can sample a diverse array of international cuisines, from Moroccan tagine to Indonesian rijsttafel, reflecting Antwerp's rich cultural tapestry and gastronomic diversity.

10.4 Ypres: World War I Memorials

Embarking on a day trip from Bruges to Ypres offers visitors a poignant journey into the heart of World War I history, where solemn memorials and historic battlefields pay tribute to the sacrifices made during the Great War. Located in the West Flanders region of Belgium, Ypres, also known as Ieper, is a somber yet captivating destination that offers a profound insight into the human cost of war and the enduring spirit of remembrance.

Getting to Ypres from Bruges:

Traveling from Bruges to Ypres is straightforward, with several transportation options available. The most common way to reach Ypres from Bruges is by train, with regular services departing from Bruges Railway Station to Ypres Railway Station. The journey typically takes around 1 hour and offers travelers a comfortable ride through the picturesque Belgian countryside. Tickets can be purchased at the station or online through the Belgian Rail website or mobile app. Alternatively, visitors can choose to travel by car, with the journey between Bruges and Ypres taking approximately 45 minutes via the E403 highway. Parking in Ypres is available at various locations throughout the city center, making it convenient for visitors to explore the area on foot or by bicycle.

Exploring Ypres' World War I Memorials:

Upon arrival in Ypres, visitors are greeted by a landscape steeped in history, with poignant memorials and historic sites scattered throughout the city and its surrounding countryside. One of the most iconic landmarks is the Menin Gate Memorial to the Missing, a solemn tribute to the thousands of soldiers who lost their lives in the Ypres Salient and have no known grave. Every evening, the Last Post ceremony is held at the Menin Gate, where buglers sound the haunting melody in remembrance of the fallen. Nearby, the In Flanders Fields Museum offers a comprehensive look at the impact of World War I on the region, with interactive exhibits and artifacts that tell the stories of soldiers, civilians, and the landscape itself. Housed in the historic Cloth Hall, the museum provides a poignant and thought-provoking experience for visitors seeking to understand the human cost of war.

Exploring the Battlefields and Cemeteries:

For those interested in exploring the battlefield sites and cemeteries of the Ypres Salient, guided tours are available that offer insight into the major battles fought in the area. Visitors can visit sites such as Hill 60, Tyne Cot Cemetery, and the Passchendaele Memorial Museum, where they can pay their respects to the fallen and gain a deeper understanding of the war's impact on the region.

Embracing Remembrance and Reflection:

As visitors wander through the streets of Ypres and its surrounding countryside, they are invited to reflect on the sacrifices made by those who fought and died in World War I. From the tranquil beauty of the war cemeteries to the haunting echoes of the battlefields, Ypres offers a poignant reminder of the human cost of conflict and the enduring importance of remembrance.

10.5 Damme: Quaint Countryside Charm

Embarking on a day trip from Bruges to Damme offers visitors a delightful escape to the serene countryside, where picturesque landscapes, historic charm, and tranquil waterways await. Located just a short distance from Bruges, Damme is a hidden gem that exudes rustic beauty and old-world charm, making it the perfect destination for travelers seeking a peaceful retreat from the bustling city.

Getting to Damme from Bruges:

Traveling from Bruges to Damme is a breeze, with several transportation options available. The most scenic way to reach Damme from Bruges is by bicycle, with a dedicated cycling path running along the picturesque Damse Vaart canal. Visitors can rent bicycles from various rental shops in Bruges and enjoy a leisurely ride through the scenic Flemish countryside, soaking in the sights and sounds of rural Belgium along the way. The cycling route to Damme is well-signposted and takes approximately 30-40 minutes, making it an enjoyable and eco-friendly way to explore the region. Alternatively, visitors can opt to travel by boat, with guided boat tours departing from Bruges and cruising along the peaceful canals to Damme. The boat ride offers a relaxing and scenic journey through the lush countryside, providing visitors with a unique perspective of the landscape and the opportunity to spot wildlife along the way. Boat tours typically take around 45 minutes to an hour, depending on the route and operator. For those preferring a quicker mode of transportation, buses also operate between Bruges and Damme, providing a convenient option for travelers seeking to maximize their time in the region. Buses depart regularly from Bruges' main bus station and arrive at Damme's central square, offering a hassle-free way to reach the quaint countryside village.

Exploring Damme's Quaint Countryside Charm:

Upon arrival in Damme, visitors are greeted by a postcard-perfect village scene, with cobblestone streets, historic buildings, and charming canal bridges dotting the landscape. One of the highlights of Damme is its well-preserved medieval architecture, including the imposing town hall and the picturesque Church of Our Lady, which dates back to the 13th century. Visitors can wander through the narrow streets and alleyways, admiring the quaint facades and soaking in the village's peaceful ambiance. Damme is also known for its thriving artisanal scene, with quaint shops and boutiques offering a variety of handmade crafts, local delicacies, and artisanal products. Visitors can browse through shops selling everything from handmade chocolates and artisanal cheeses to unique souvenirs and handcrafted goods, providing the perfect opportunity to pick up a memento of their visit to Damme.

Embracing Outdoor Activities:

For nature enthusiasts and outdoor adventurers, Damme offers plenty of opportunities to explore the surrounding countryside and enjoy outdoor activities such as hiking, cycling, and boating. The region is crisscrossed with scenic walking and cycling trails, offering stunning views of the countryside and the chance to spot wildlife such as birds, rabbits, and even deer. Visitors can also rent paddleboats or kayaks and explore the tranquil canals at their own pace, immersing themselves in the beauty of nature and enjoying a peaceful escape from the hustle and bustle of city life.

Indulging in Culinary Delights:

No visit to Damme would be complete without sampling the local culinary delights, and the village boasts a variety of charming cafes, restaurants, and taverns where visitors can enjoy traditional Belgian dishes and regional specialties.

CHAPTER 11

ENTERTAINMENT AND NIGHTLIFE

11.1 Bars and Pubs

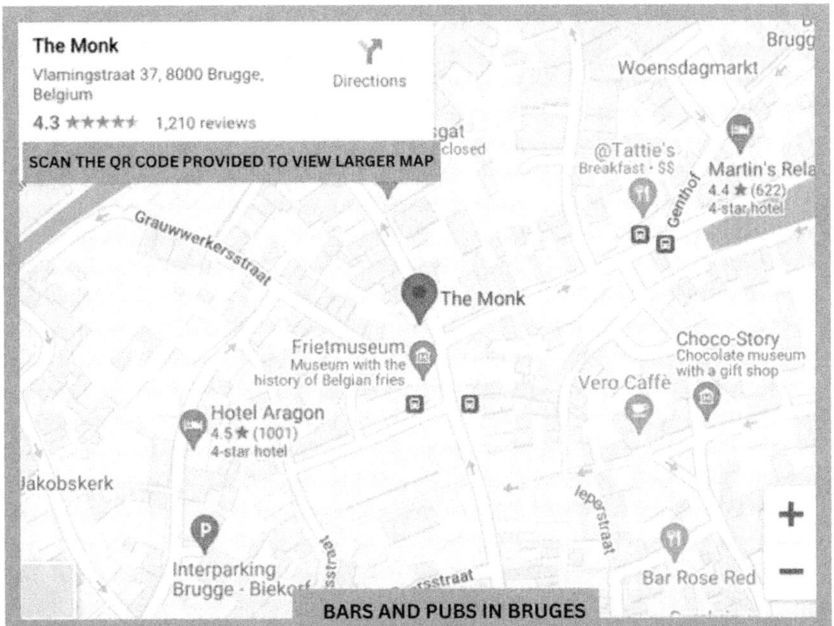

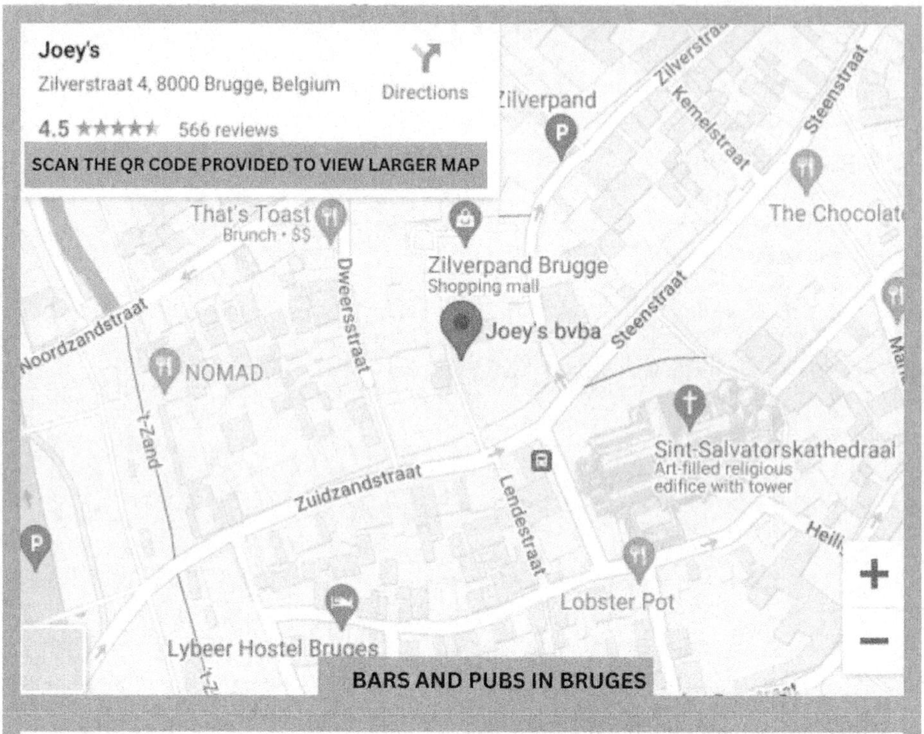
Joey's
Zilverstraat 4, 8000 Brugge, Belgium
Directions
4.5 566 reviews
SCAN THE QR CODE PROVIDED TO VIEW LARGER MAP
Zilverpand
Zilverstraat
Kemelstraat
Steenstraat
The Chocolat
That's Toast
Brunch · $$
Dweersstraat
Zilverpand Brugge
Shopping mall
Joey's bvba
Steenstraat
Noordzandstraat
NOMAD
't Zand
Sint-Salvatorskathedraal
Art-filled religious
edifice with tower
Zuidzandstraat
Lendestraat
Lobster Pot
Lybeer Hostel Bruges
BARS AND PUBS IN BRUGES

SCAN THE QR CODE PROVIDED TO VIEW LARGER MAP
Scan the QR Code with a device to view a comprehensive and larger map of Bars and Pubs in Bruges
BARS AND PUBS IN BRUGES

In the heart of Bruges, amidst its cobblestone streets and historic buildings, lies a vibrant bar scene waiting to be discovered. From cozy pubs serving traditional Belgian brews to stylish cocktail bars with innovative concoctions, Bruges offers something for every palate and preference.

't Brugs Beertje:

Nestled in the city center, 't Brugs Beertje is a beloved institution among beer enthusiasts, offering an extensive selection of Belgian brews in a cozy, traditional setting. With over 300 different beers to choose from, including rare and hard-to-find varieties, 't Brugs Beertje is a paradise for beer connoisseurs looking to explore the rich diversity of Belgian beer culture. Prices typically range from €4 to €8 per beer, depending on the brew's rarity and complexity. The bar opens daily from 4:00 PM to 1:00 AM, providing ample opportunity for visitors to indulge in a leisurely tasting session. With its warm ambiance, knowledgeable staff, and exceptional beer selection, 't Brugs Beertje offers a quintessential Belgian drinking experience.

Le Trappiste:

Located just a stone's throw from the iconic Belfry of Bruges, Le Trappiste is a charming bar specializing in Trappist beers brewed by monks in monasteries across Belgium. The bar features an impressive selection of Trappist ales, including famous brands such as Westvleteren, Chimay, and Orval, as well as lesser-known gems waiting to be discovered. Prices for Trappist beers typically range from €4 to €10, depending on the brand and rarity. Le Trappiste opens its doors daily from 2:00 PM to 2:00 AM, welcoming visitors to savor the unique flavors of Trappist beer in a cozy, candlelit atmosphere. With its authentic ambiance and curated beer selection, Le Trappiste is a must-visit destination for beer enthusiasts seeking a taste of Belgian brewing tradition.

Groot Vlaenderen:

Housed in a beautifully restored 17th-century building, Groot Vlaenderen exudes old-world charm and elegance, offering visitors a sophisticated setting to enjoy a wide range of beverages. The bar boasts an extensive selection of Belgian beers, wines, and spirits, as well as an impressive cocktail menu featuring both classic and innovative creations. Prices at Groot Vlaenderen are slightly higher than average, with beers ranging from €5 to €10 and cocktails priced between €10 and €15. The bar opens daily from 4:00 PM to 1:00 AM, providing guests with the perfect ambiance for a pre-dinner aperitif or a late-night cocktail. With its historic setting, attentive service, and refined atmosphere, Groot Vlaenderen offers a memorable drinking experience in the heart of Bruges' historic center.

De Garre:

Tucked away down a narrow alleyway near the Markt square, De Garre is a hidden gem beloved by locals and visitors alike for its cozy ambiance and exceptional selection of house beers. The bar is renowned for its signature tripel beer, brewed exclusively for De Garre by the nearby Brouwerij Van Steenberge. Poured from the tap into traditional ceramic glasses, De Garre Tripel is a must-try for beer enthusiasts seeking a taste of authentic Belgian brewing. Prices at De Garre are reasonable, with the house tripel priced at around €5 per glass. The bar opens daily from 11:00 AM to 12:00 AM, with limited seating available due to its popularity. Despite its hidden location, De Garre is well worth seeking out for a unique and memorable drinking experience in Bruges.

Bar des Amis:

Situated in the bustling Simon Stevinplein square, Bar des Amis is a lively neighborhood bar known for its welcoming atmosphere and diverse clientele. The bar offers a selection of Belgian beers, wines, and spirits, as well as a menu of light snacks and appetizers. Prices at Bar des Amis are reasonable, with beers starting at €3.50 and cocktails priced between €8 and €12. The bar opens daily from 3:00 PM to 1:00 AM, providing guests with ample opportunity to unwind and socialize with friends old and new. With its friendly staff, laid-back vibe, and prime location, Bar des Amis is the perfect spot to relax and enjoy the company of fellow travelers and locals alike.

The Monk:

For those seeking a contemporary take on Belgian beer culture, The Monk offers a stylish and innovative drinking experience in the heart of Bruges. The bar features a rotating selection of craft beers from local and international breweries, as well as a curated list of artisanal cocktails and spirits. Prices at The Monk vary depending on the beer or cocktail chosen, with beers typically ranging from €4 to €8 and cocktails priced between €10 and €15. The bar opens daily from 5:00 PM to 1:00 AM, welcoming guests to enjoy its sleek, modern ambiance and creative libations. With its eclectic drink menu and trendy atmosphere, The Monk appeals to a younger crowd looking to explore the cutting edge of Bruges' bar scene.

11.2 Live Music Venues

In the enchanting city of Bruges, music fills the air, beckoning visitors to experience the lively and diverse live music scene that thrives within its historic streets. From cozy cafes hosting intimate acoustic sessions to bustling bars pulsating with the rhythm of live bands, Bruges offers a plethora of venues where music enthusiasts can immerse themselves in captivating performances and unforgettable experiences.

The Old Slaughterhouse:

Located in a converted 19th-century slaughterhouse, The Old Slaughterhouse is a unique live music venue that seamlessly blends Bruges' rich history with its vibrant cultural scene. With its exposed brick walls, vaulted ceilings, and industrial-chic decor, the venue provides a captivating backdrop for an eclectic lineup of musical performances, ranging from jazz and blues to rock and indie. Visitors can enjoy live music acts several nights a week, with performances typically starting around 8:00 PM. The Old Slaughterhouse also boasts a cozy bar serving a selection of Belgian beers and artisanal cocktails, making it the perfect spot to unwind and enjoy a night of music and merriment.

De Republiek:

Situated in a historic building that once served as a cinema and cultural center, De Republiek is a vibrant hub for arts and entertainment in the heart of Bruges. The venue hosts an array of live music events throughout the year, ranging from intimate acoustic sets to lively performances by local and international bands. With its eclectic programming and welcoming atmosphere, De Republiek attracts music lovers of all ages and tastes, creating a dynamic and inclusive community of artists and audiences. Visitors can check the venue's website or social media pages for upcoming events and ticket information, ensuring they don't miss out on the opportunity to experience the magic of live music at De Republiek.

De Kelk:

Nestled in a quaint corner of Bruges' historic center, De Kelk is a charming cafe-bar known for its intimate atmosphere and regular live music performances, particularly in the folk and acoustic genres. With its warm wooden interiors, flickering candlelight, and welcoming ambiance, De Kelk provides the perfect setting for musicians to showcase their talents and for audiences to unwind and enjoy the music. Live music sessions are typically held on weekends, starting around 9:00 PM, allowing visitors to relax with a drink in hand and soak in the soothing sounds of acoustic melodies and heartfelt lyrics.

Whether you're a folk music enthusiast or simply seeking a cozy spot to enjoy live music in Bruges, De Kelk promises an unforgettable experience.

Cafe Vlissinghe:

Founded in 1515, Cafe Vlissinghe is one of the oldest pubs in Bruges, steeped in centuries of history and tradition. Beyond its historic facade and cozy interiors lies a hidden gem for music lovers, with the pub hosting regular live music sessions featuring local musicians and bands. Visitors can enjoy performances ranging from traditional folk music to contemporary covers, all within the timeless ambiance of this historic establishment. Live music events are typically held on select evenings, starting around 8:00 PM, providing the perfect opportunity to sample Belgian beers and immerse yourself in the rich musical heritage of Bruges' oldest pub.

The Groot Vlaenderen Jazz Club:

For jazz aficionados seeking an authentic live music experience, The Groot Vlaenderen Jazz Club is a must-visit destination in Bruges. Located in a historic building with a rich cultural heritage, the club hosts regular jazz performances by talented local and international musicians, spanning a wide range of styles and influences. Visitors can expect to be transported back in time to the golden age of jazz, with performances that evoke the spirit of legends such as Louis Armstrong, Duke Ellington, and Ella Fitzgerald. The club's intimate setting and attentive audience create a magical atmosphere where music truly comes alive, making it a favorite haunt for jazz lovers and music enthusiasts alike.

11.3 Theater and Performance Arts

In the heart of Bruges, a city steeped in history and culture, lies a vibrant and thriving performing arts scene that captivates audiences with its diverse array of theatrical productions, musical performances, and dance recitals. From historic theaters to contemporary performance spaces, Bruges offers visitors a wealth of opportunities to immerse themselves in the magic of live entertainment and experience the city's rich cultural heritage firsthand.

Theaterzaal Sirkel:

Located in the heart of Bruges' historic center, Theaterzaal Sirkel is a dynamic cultural venue that showcases a wide range of theatrical productions, including plays, musicals, and dance performances. With its state-of-the-art facilities and intimate seating arrangement, Theaterzaal Sirkel offers audiences an immersive and engaging theater experience that brings stories to life on stage. Ticket prices vary depending on the production and seating arrangement, with discounts available for students and seniors. The theater typically opens its doors in the evening, with performances starting around 8:00 PM, providing visitors with the perfect opportunity to enjoy a night of entertainment in the heart of Bruges.

Concertgebouw Brugge:

Situated on 't Zand square, Concertgebouw Brugge is a prestigious cultural institution that celebrates music, dance, and the performing arts. The venue hosts a diverse program of concerts, recitals, and theatrical performances throughout the year, featuring renowned artists and emerging talents from around the world. Ticket prices for events at Concertgebouw Brugge vary depending on the performance and seating category, with discounts available for members and subscribers. The venue opens its doors in the late afternoon, with performances scheduled throughout the evening, allowing visitors to enjoy a wide range of cultural experiences in one of Bruges' most iconic buildings.

Stadsschouwburg Brugge:

Dating back to the 19th century, Stadsschouwburg Brugge is a historic theater that serves as a focal point for the performing arts in Bruges. With its ornate architecture and rich history, the theater provides a stunning backdrop for a diverse program of theatrical productions, including dramas, comedies, and classical performances. Ticket prices for shows at Stadsschouwburg Brugge vary depending on the production and seating category, with discounts available for students and groups. The theater typically opens its doors in the early evening, with performances starting around 7:30 PM, offering visitors the opportunity to experience the magic of live theater in a truly historic setting.

De Werf:

Situated along the banks of the Dijver canal, De Werf is a contemporary cultural center that celebrates the performing arts in all their forms. The venue hosts a diverse range of events, including theater productions, dance performances, and experimental performances by local and international artists. Ticket prices for events at De Werf vary depending on the performance and seating arrangement, with discounts available for members and subscribers. The center opens its doors in the late afternoon, with performances scheduled throughout the evening, providing visitors with the chance to experience cutting-edge performances in a modern and innovative setting.

De Biekorf:

Nestled in the heart of Bruges' historic city center, De Biekorf is a cultural center that celebrates the arts in all their forms, including theater, music, and visual arts. The venue hosts a diverse program of events, ranging from theatrical productions and musical performances to film screenings and art exhibitions. Ticket prices for events at De Biekorf vary depending on the performance and seating arrangement, with discounts available for students and seniors. The center typically opens its doors in the early evening, with events scheduled throughout the night, providing visitors with the opportunity to immerse themselves in the vibrant cultural scene of Bruges.

11.4 Nightclubs and Dance Halls

In the charming city of Bruges, where historic architecture meets modern vibrancy, the nightlife scene comes alive with an array of nightclubs and dance halls offering visitors the chance to dance until dawn. From chic clubs pulsating with electronic beats to lively venues hosting live bands and DJs, Bruges offers something for every nightlife enthusiast.

Club De B:

Nestled in the heart of Bruges' historic center, Club De B is a premier nightclub known for its energetic atmosphere and eclectic music selection. With its sleek and modern interior, state-of-the-art sound system, and dynamic lighting effects, Club De B provides the perfect backdrop for a night of dancing and revelry. The club hosts a variety of themed nights and special events, featuring top local and international DJs spinning the latest electronic and dance tracks. Entry prices typically range from €10 to €20, depending on the night and any special events. Club De B is open on Fridays and Saturdays from 11:00 PM to 6:00 AM, ensuring that partygoers can dance into the early hours of the morning in style.

Café Charlatan:

Located just a short walk from Bruges' historic Markt square, Café Charlatan is a beloved nightlife destination that combines the charm of a cozy cafe with the energy of a bustling dance hall. With its eclectic decor, laid-back vibe, and diverse music lineup, Café Charlatan attracts a diverse crowd of locals and tourists alike. The venue hosts live bands and DJs playing everything from indie rock and alternative to funk and soul, ensuring that there's something for everyone to enjoy. Entry to Café Charlatan is typically free or low-cost, with drinks priced reasonably. The venue is open on select nights from around 9:00 PM until the early hours of the morning, offering visitors the chance to dance and mingle until dawn in a welcoming and inclusive atmosphere.

Entrenous:

Situated in a historic building along Bruges' picturesque canals, Entrenous is a sophisticated nightclub that combines elegant surroundings with pulsating beats. With its chic and stylish interior, VIP lounges, and top-of-the-line sound system, Entrenous provides a luxurious setting for a night out on the town. The club hosts a variety of themed nights and special events, featuring a mix of live performances and DJ sets spanning genres such as house, techno, and R&B. Entry prices at Entrenous vary depending on the night and any special events, with drinks priced accordingly. The club is open on weekends from around 11:00 PM to 6:00 AM, offering visitors the chance to experience the height of Bruges' nightlife in an exclusive and upscale setting.

Club 55:

Situated on the outskirts of Bruges, Club 55 is a sprawling nightclub complex that boasts multiple dance floors, bars, and outdoor terraces, ensuring that the party never stops. With its expansive layout and cutting-edge design, Club 55 offers visitors a truly immersive nightlife experience, with a diverse lineup of DJs and live performers keeping the dance floors packed until the early hours of the morning. Entry prices at Club 55 vary depending on the night and any special events, with VIP packages available for those looking to elevate their experience. The club is open on Fridays and Saturdays from 10:00 PM until the sun comes up, providing partygoers with the ultimate nocturnal playground in Bruges.

The Crash:

Tucked away in a converted warehouse on the outskirts of Bruges, The Crash is a haven for fans of alternative music and underground subculture. With its gritty industrial setting, underground vibe, and cutting-edge music lineup, The Crash offers a unique and immersive nightlife experience that appeals to the city's edgier crowd. The venue hosts a variety of themed nights and special events, featuring live bands, DJs, and performance artists pushing the boundaries of creativity and expression. Entry prices at The Crash are typically low-cost, with drinks priced reasonably. The venue is open on select nights from around 9:00 PM until the early hours of the morning, providing visitors with a glimpse into Bruges' thriving alternative scene.

CONCLUSION AND RECOMMENDATIONS

As we come to the final pages of the "Bruges Comprehensive Travel Guide 2024," I invite you to reflect on the journey we've embarked upon together – a journey filled with wonder, discovery, and endless fascination. Within these pages, I've shared a treasure trove of insights, recommendations, and insider tips to help you navigate the enchanting city of Bruges and unlock its many secrets. As you prepare to embark on your own adventure to Bruges, allow me to offer a few final recommendations to ensure that your experience is nothing short of magical:

Get Lost in the Old Town: Embrace the spirit of exploration by wandering through the medieval streets of Bruges' Old Town. Lose yourself in its labyrinthine alleys, discover hidden courtyards, and stumble upon charming cafes and boutique shops tucked away from the main thoroughfares.

Sample the Local Delicacies: Indulge your taste buds with the culinary delights of Bruges, from crispy frites dipped in creamy mayonnaise to decadent Belgian chocolates and mouthwatering waffles. Be sure to visit the city's traditional beer halls and sample a variety of locally brewed beers, each with its own unique flavor and character.

Climb the Belfry for Panoramic Views: For a bird's-eye view of Bruges and its picturesque surroundings, climb to the top of the iconic Belfry tower. From its lofty heights, you'll be treated to panoramic vistas of the city skyline, the winding canals, and the verdant countryside beyond.

Explore Beyond the City Limits: While Bruges itself is a treasure trove of history and culture, don't hesitate to venture beyond its borders to explore the surrounding region. Take a day trip to the charming village of Damme, cycle along the scenic canal paths, or visit the nearby coastal town of Knokke-Heist for a day of sun, sand, and sea.

Engage with the Locals: The true heart of Bruges lies in its people – warm, welcoming, and eager to share their love for their city. Strike up a conversation with a local, whether it's at a cozy cafe, a bustling market, or a lively street festival. You'll gain valuable insights and forge connections that will enrich your experience.

In closing, I extend my heartfelt gratitude to you, dear reader, for joining me on this journey through the timeless streets of Bruges. May the experiences we have shared inspire you to embark on your own adventure to this magical city, where history comes alive, and every moment is filled with wonder. Whether you are a seasoned traveler or setting out on your very first expedition, may Bruges capture your heart and leave an indelible mark on your soul.

Printed in Great Britain
by Amazon

44071215R00086